Revival Fire
and Glory

A Baptist Minister Recounts His Experiences

with a NEW WAVE of God's Glory

D1056454

by
Bob Shattles

McDougal Publishing is a ministry of The McDougal Foundation, Inc., a Maryland nonprofit corporation dedicated to spreading the Gospel of the Lord Jesus Christ to as many people as possible in the shortest time possible.

Published by:

McDougal Publishing
P.O. Box 3595
Hagerstown, MD 21742-3595
www.mcdougal.org

ISBN 1-884369-84-7

Printed in the United States of America
For Worldwide Distribution

I dictated some of the stories for this book into a tape recorder as I traveled one day from Austell to Brunswick, Georgia in my car. I was all alone, but as I spoke of the blessings of God that we are experiencing, gold dust began to fall in the car. It covered my face, it was all over the dashboard, and it was all over the tape recorder. I could feel the heat of the Spirit in my body and in my hands as I drove along the highways toward my destination. Oil came from my hands and got on the steering wheel. I sensed that God was saying that this book was appointed and anointed by Him and that He would use it for His glory.

This is our prayer as well.

Bob Shattles

DEDICATION

I dedicate this book:

To my wife, MARY FAULKNER SHATTLES, who has stood by me and encouraged me now since 1957.

To my children, JIM and ROBYN, and my grandchildren, whom I love with all my heart.

To my brother, BILL SHATTLES, and his family, who labor with me in *Revival Fires* at Friendship Baptist Church.

To all the Friendship church family, without whom *Revival Fire* could not possibly burn in our church.

To my hero, my daddy, WILLIAM PAUL SHATTLES, and my mama, JANICE MARIE CARTER SHATTLES, who taught me the values of the Christian life and the way folks ought to live.

ACKNOWLEDGMENTS

I must say a hearty thank you to Harold McDougal and the staff of McDougal Publishing. Without their help, I might never have been able to finish this book. I believe the book will bless many. I thank them for helping me pull it together, and I thank God for people with a servant's heart.

I thank Jim and Cathy Durley and their daughters, Chrisi and Jayme, for their work on the book and their financial contribution toward its production.

Many thanks to my wife Mary and my daughter and son, Robyn and Jim, for all the time spent confirming dates and events that happened to us as a family.

I thank my brother Bill for helping me to remember the details of the many miracles God has given us and for being willing to work with me to perfect the manuscript.

Last, but not least, I am thankful to Ruth Ward Heflin for her encouragement, her facilitation of the project and her review of the manuscript.

And He [Jesus] said to them, "Go into all the world and preach the gospel to all creation. He who has believed and has been baptized shall be saved; but he who has disbelieved shall be condemned.

"And these signs will accompany those who have believed: in My name they will cast out demons, they will speak with new tongues; they will pick up serpents, and if they drink any deadly poison, it shall not hurt them; they will lay hands on the sick, and they will recover."

So then, when the Lord Jesus had spoken to them, He was received up into heaven, and sat down at the right hand of God. And they went out and preached everywhere, while the Lord worked with them, and confirmed the word by the signs that followed. Mark 16:15-20

CONTENTS

Foreword by Pastor Bill Ligon

Bob Shattles has been a good pastor for a very long time. He has taken his call seriously since the day God led him to resign from the Atlanta Police Department to pastor a church. Over a period of many years, he has successfully taken small congregations and helped them grow into big ones, and many people will be in Heaven because he went to them, no matter where they were, to tell them about Jesus.

Now, however, an entirely new phase has come into Pastor Bob's ministry. Suddenly, signs and wonders, just like those recorded in the book of Acts, are manifesting themselves wherever he preaches. I have personally witnessed a golden rain coming down in his services and a miraculous anointing oil pouring forth from his hands. These signs and wonders are attracting people from far and near, as signs did with the original apostles of the Church. People are coming from everywhere just to be near this man and to witness the visible outpouring of God's love upon him.

Just as with the first apostles, signs are following Brother Bob's preaching, and just as with the early apostles, people in large numbers are being encouraged to follow Jesus.

Jesus said, *"The works that I do shall [you] do also"* (John 14:12, KJV), and it is time for the works of Jesus to be present in the Church to demonstrate the power of God.

The fruit of Bob Shattles' ministry is good. This is the reason I have had him preaching revival now for the past twelve weeks in my church. I am so glad that God has allowed me to be the host pastor and my church to be the host church for this modern-day revival with signs and wonders.

Bill Ligon
Pastor, Christian Renewal Church
Brunswick, Georgia

FOREWORD BY RUTH WARD HEFLIN

Two weeks before Thanksgiving of 1998 I received a telephone call from Pastor Bob Shattles from Georgia. He said my name had been in his spirit and that God had told him that if I would come to his church, He would bring him and his church into a new realm of the glory of God. When I asked him where he was located, he said he was west of Atlanta, and since I was scheduled to be in another church in Atlanta that following Thursday, I suggested that I come to his church on that Tuesday and Wednesday. I had reserved several days to be home, but because he and his people were so hungry for God, I was willing to go — if it was not too short a notice for them. They were willing, he said.

I found both Brother Bob Shattles and his people to be very warm and loving, and we had some wonderful services together. The first night I ministered, Pastor Shattles was carried away to Heaven and had supernatural oil appear in his hands. It must have been at least a quarter of a cup or more, and he had to keep his hands cupped because of the oil that was accumulating in his palms. The next morning, the oil was there again, and he began to anoint the people who were present in the service.

11

On Wednesday night, I looked over at him, and there was gold dust on his face and neck. God was doing something new and wonderful.

On Thanksgiving Day I called Austell to see how things were going, and I first got the church answering service. What I heard on the recorded message was so dynamic that it thrilled my soul: "This is Pastor Bob Shattles of Friendship Baptist Church. Come on over because we are in the midst of revival, the glory of God is falling upon us as gold dust and supernatural oil, and God is doing mighty miracles in our midst." I had never heard an answering machine message quite like that, and I called several friends, gave them the number and suggested that they call and listen for themselves. I knew that they would experience revival, just hearing what Bob had to say.

When I located Bob's home number and called him there, he began to tell me what had happened since I was with them. It was phenomenal. Gold dust had been raining down from Heaven upon the service, and his people had all seen it. Some had found it in their hair when they were getting ready to go back to church that Sunday night. How exciting it all was for me, too!

Several months later, when I was in France, God spoke to me to go and spend several days with Pastor Shattles. Just as soon as we could arrange it, I flew in to be with him in the revival he had begun in Brunswick, Georgia, with Pastor Bill Ligon and his congregation at Christian Renewal Center. The first night, as I sat on the platform, I was amazed to see gold dust raining down upon the platform four or five times during the first twenty minutes of the service. My associate, Ruth Carneal, was seated in the audience, and I quickly called for her to come forward to see what I was seeing. Later I had to tell Pastor Ligon that I was raised correctly and that I did know the pulpit etiquette of not inviting people onto someone else's platform. What was happening had been so unusual that I had spontaneously called for her, not wanting her to miss it.

Since that time, Pastor Bob and I have been on several telecasts together, he has preached for us at our Men's Convention in Ashland, and we did a camp-meeting together near Dallas, Texas. He continues to move in *Revival Fire and Glory*, and I sense that what is happening in his life and ministry is the new wave of revival, the new wave of God's glory among us.

Ruth Ward Heflin
Ashland, Virginia

INTRODUCTION

I was born into a cotton-mill family on my daddy's side and into a florist-farm family on my mama's side. All my family were poor people, and all of them were Baptists. I'm a Baptist too, and I believe in everything the Baptist name stands for. I have come to realize, however, that over the years we Baptists have lost a very important part of our ministry, a part that we desperately need to have restored. It is the work of the Holy Spirit in the midst of us.

Don't get me wrong. I'm proud of Baptists. We are the greatest soul-winners in all the world. If we could just add to our soul-winning zeal the power of the Holy Spirit and the truth of God's Word with faith in its fullness, we would have a combination that would rock the world in these last days. That's what I want to see, and that's why I'm writing this book.

I'm not hung up on denomination. Denominations are not nearly as important as some of us try to make them. God is breaking down denominational barriers all over the world and bringing His children into a full harmonious relationship with Him and with each other as one body. This is the Church, the Bride for which Jesus will return. It will be wonderful when we can all love one another, and we'd better prepare for it. He is coming sooner than we imagine. To prepare us quickly, the Lord is sending revival fire upon us, and recently He has added to those revival fire His glory. We are now experiencing a new wave of the power of God, *Revival Fire and Glory.*

I pray that this book will touch the hearts and lives of God's people everywhere. May you see that God is more powerful than tradition, that His Word is more powerful than anything that men could possibly devise. And may you know that He is ready to bless YOU and to do it TODAY.

Bob Shattles
Austell, Georgia

Chapter

One

"With Glistening Gold"

When you lie down among the sheepfolds, You are like the wings of a dove covered with silver, And its pinions with glistening gold.
                                        Psalm 68:13

WHEN I GOT UP THAT SUNDAY MORNING, THERE WAS supernatural oil on my hands and gold dust on my clothing. I went to the church and preached, and gold dust began to fall so heavily in the sanctuary of Friendship Baptist Church that everyone present saw it too.

Patsy Burton, one of our sisters, picked up two pieces of gold from the carpet that morning, put them on a piece of Scotch tape, and taped them inside her Bible. It was as much from curiosity as from anything else.

What was this strange substance that was suddenly appearing in our midst? Would it last? Or would it quickly disappear? Would it somehow change over time? This experience was so new to us that we had no answers to these questions. It was such a new experience that we were all still getting used to it.

A day or two later, Patsy was in the hospital, visiting a friend of hers who had a large cancerous tumor on the back of her hand. The fear of her doctors was that the roots of it had already extended into other parts of her body.

Patsy was telling this lady about what was happening in our services, and she opened her Bible and showed her the gold. "There is such a great anointing upon this gold," she told her, "that sometimes when I open my Bible to read, I feel drunk in the Spirit."

"Well, take it out and put it on this tumor," the lady said, "and let's see what happens." So Patsy took the piece of Scotch tape with the two pieces of gold dust on it and placed it over the tumor. Sometime during the next five or ten minutes, as the two of them sat there and talked, the tumor completely disappeared.

The lady had been scheduled for surgery the following morning. When it became obvious that there had been a remarkable change in her condition, her doctors tested her again and found that all signs of her cancer had disappeared. They said these words: "This had to be God." Six months later, there is still no sign of that cancer. It has not reappeared, and we give all the glory to God.

Patsy works for a drugstore in our area, and it just so happened that at the time this miraculous manifestation began the pharmacist's wife was in serious condition, in a coma in the Intensive Care Unit of the local hospital. Doctors did not expect her to live. When the pharmacist heard about the miracle God had done through Patsy in the hospital, he asked her if she would pray for his wife. To our knowledge he was not a saved man, but Patsy took a prayer cloth from the church to him, and he, in turn, took it to the hospital for his wife.

Several days later, when the pharmacist came into the workplace, he was ecstatic. When Patsy asked him why he was so happy, he said that his wife had come out of the coma and was beginning to recover. She recovered fully, and several of her family members were saved as a result of this miracle.

Other members of our church were also experiencing the gold dust. Mary Miller told me that first

Sunday evening that when she was combing her hair, getting ready for the service, gold dust began to fall from her hair. It had been there apparently since the morning service.

Another of our members, who is himself an evangelist and pastor, said that gold dust appeared in his house. Many of our people showed me gold dust that was appearing on them, too. It was appearing everywhere.

The big question on everyone's mind was: WHERE IS THIS FOUND IN THE BIBLE? I wanted to know too, so I asked the Lord. He gave me the answer through the 68th Psalm. The Church is a sheepfold because that's where the sheep gather. That's where the Great Shepherd, the Lord God Almighty, ministers to His sheep. He said:

> *When you lie down among the sheepfolds, You are like the wings of a dove covered with silver, And its pinions with glistening gold.*
>
> Psalm 68:13

That took care of the gold (as far as I was concerned), but what about the oil? I found the answer in the book of Zechariah:

> *Then said I to him, "What are these two olive trees on the right of the lampstand and on its left?" And I answered the second time and said*

> *to him, "What are the two olive branches which*
> *are beside the two golden pipes, which empty*
> *the golden oil from themselves?"*
> *So he answered me, saying, "Do you not know*
> *what these are?"*
> *And I said, "No, my lord."*
> *Then he said, "These are the two anointed ones*
> *who are standing by the Lord of the whole*
> *earth."*   Zechariah 4:11-14

This phrase *"the anointed ones"* literally means "the sons of fresh oil." God is revealing His glory upon us by sending us fresh oil. It is a sign of His presence.

What is clear in the Scriptures is that God desires to reveal Himself to us through many signs and wonders. Jesus Himself said that signs and wonders would follow His disciples, His apostles, the believers, and He did not necessarily specify what all those signs and wonders would be.

Great signs and wonders followed His own ministry, and we cannot say for sure that He did not Himself experience these particular manifestations. It is very possible that He did, for the Word of God declares:

> *Therefore many other signs Jesus also per-*
> *formed in the presence of the disciples, which*
> *are not written in this book.*   John 20:30

> *And there are also many other things which Je-*
> *sus did, which if they were written in detail, I*
> *suppose that even the world itself would not*
> *contain the books that would be written.*
>
> John 21:25

I had no more questions for the Lord. By faith, I was ready to accept anything and everything that He was doing. I was just thinking, "There's an anointing in this, and I want it to flow in me, in my ministry, and in my home."

My journey of faith had brought me to a very exciting and very fruitful new level.

Chapter

Two

"The Way He Should Go"

Train up a child in the way he should go, Even when he is old he will not depart from it.

Proverbs 22:6

MY LIFE OF FAITH HAD BEGUN IN A LITTLE BAPTIST CHURCH in Cobb County, Georgia, when I was only eight years old.

I was born in Fulton Bag Cotton Mill Village, a poor section of Atlanta. Granddaddy Shattles worked in the mill there. He was also Chairman of Deacons at Immanuel Baptist Church. Grandmama Shattles was a Sunday school teacher and head of the Women's Missionary Union. Our grandparents gave God all they had.

The Shattles clan was a large one, with thirteen children and a whole mess of grandchildren and great-grandchildren. We were reportedly descended from some brothers who came over from Ireland, but we also had Cherokee blood in our family (from both sides) and several other nationalities mixed in. We were Americans, Georgians and Baptists.

Since the Shattles had such a large family, I had many other children to grow up with. Aunt Dorothy, for example, was just three years older than I was, so we were more like siblings.

Although we were poor, our grandparents were very generous and would feed anyone who needed help. I remember my grandfather scraping around to get enough for Grandmama to buy a new pair of shoes. Instead of her buying a new pair of shoes for herself, she bought shoes for someone else. Then she put some new cardboard in her own shoes and used them a while longer. That was very typical of our grandparents. They were like that. We used a whole lot of cardboard in our shoes in those days.

Mama made my shirts from flour sacks. The bad thing about being just under Dorothy in age was that, because she was a girl, I couldn't take advantage of her hand-me-downs. Still I never knew we were poor until someone told me after I grew up. Poverty is what you make of it. I thought we were pretty well off. When we have a personal relationship with the Lord Jesus Christ, we are never poor. Because our family loved the Lord and loved one another, we thought we were rich, and we were.

Every Friday, when Granddaddy came home from his work at the mill, all of us kids would gather out in front of the house, and he would give each of us a nickel. With tokens we got from the flour sacks, we were able to get into the movies, and with the nickel Granddaddy gave us, we could buy a candy bar or a bag of popcorn. Once you got into the movie house, you could stay all day if you wanted, so sometimes on Saturdays, we sat and watched Tom Mix, Hopalong Cassidy, Roy Rogers and Gene Autry in their western musicals. It was all pretty clean entertainment.

We were taught to share at our house, but when it came to candy, we were not as generous in our sharing. Candy came along so rarely that we tried to keep it to ourselves and stretch it out as long as we could.

Once, when I had the mumps and could not be there when Granddaddy came home to get my weekly nickel, he gave it to Dorothy and told her to give it to me. She did, but then she offered to go to the store a block away and get both of us some candy. I gave her back the nickel, and she went to buy the candy. I always believed afterward that she purposely bought the sourest candy she could find, knowing that I would not be able to eat it, and then she could have it all for herself. We often laughed about it in the years to come.

The influence our grandparents had on our lives in those formative years was immense. We either lived in the house with them, next door to them or across the street from them, and most of what we knew of God they taught us.

Our grandparents raised us well. There was never a question, for example, about us going to church. We all went, and we always went, and that was that. Most every Sunday, after the service, the preacher would come home with us for Sunday dinner.

Both our grandparents and our parents believed firmly in the promise of the Bible: *"Train up a child in the way he should go, Even when he is old he will not depart from it"* (Proverbs 22:6). They were sure that although children might stray from their spiritual roots, they would always come back in later life.

When the war started and Daddy had to go to the South Pacific, Mama moved us to Cobb County to a farm owned by her parents. Grandmama Carter was a fine Christian lady who always went to church and had been saved as a small girl. Granddaddy Carter had some fine Christian ways, but I don't think he ever understood what it meant to be saved. He never went to church at least, although he did eventually accept the Lord before he died.

In Cobb County, we attended Mt. Pisgah Baptist Church. The old church had no electric lights inside and no plumbing, but people worshiped God there, and many found Christ at those old tearstained altars.

The first summer we were in Cobb County, Pastor Will Barnes had a revival. I don't remember the name of the evangelist who came to preach that revival, but I do remember that on the last night of the revival, when the altar call was given, I stood at my pew crying, knowing that I should go forward. The Spirit of God was tugging at my heart, showing me that this was my day of salvation. I stood there for the longest time in that state, as the congregation sang *"O, Why Not Tonight?"*

The service ended, and I still hadn't gone forward, but I had not moved from my place. I was still standing there crying.

Most of the people filed out, but an elderly deacon, a man who later became a preacher and started a full-Gospel church, saw what was happening with me and came over to see if he could help me. His name was Bob Cole, and he and his brothers owned a dairy farm.

"What's the matter, son?" he inquired, "Why are you crying?"

"I was supposed to get saved tonight," I answered, "but I didn't go down."

That precious man of God, who went home to be with Jesus many years ago, quickly ran outside to find the pastor. He understood that a soul hung in the balance, and that my eternal fate was being decided.

Pastor Barnes was standing outside the church talking with some of the people. Brother Cole asked him if he and the others could come back in and resume the service so that I could get saved. Would they sing that hymn one more time?

The people filed back in and took their places, and Pastor Barnes led everyone in that old hymn one more time: *"Wilt thou be saved? O, why not tonight?"*

I wasn't about to lose my opportunity again. As our friends and neighbors sang, I made my way down the aisle to the altar. There I knelt and prayed and invited Jesus to come into my heart and to be the Lord of my life. I was gloriously saved that night, redeemed by the precious blood of the Lord Jesus Christ. And from that day until I went into the army at the age of nineteen, I never missed a single church service.

Chapter

Three

"A Dog Returns to Its Own Vomit"

It has happened to them according to the true proverb, "A dog returns to its own vomit," and, "A sow, after washing, returns to wallowing in the mire."　　　　2 Peter 2:22

GRANDDADDY CARTER WAS A KIND MAN, BUT FIRM. HE believed that children should do their part, and I had to work on the farm. That hard work never hurt me, and I believe we could use a little of it with our children today.

Besides working in the fields, I was expected to cut and split wood, bring in wood and coal for the heating fire in winter and build a fire in the old wood stove in the kitchen so that Grandmama could cook.

Even when I got home from school in the afternoon, I was expected to go to the fields and work.

When I got into high school, I discovered that I had an aptitude for sports, and I loved it, especially baseball and football. I was six-foot-one, weighed a hundred and ninety pounds and had kept myself in good physical condition through work on the farm. It also helped that I had never started drinking or smoking.

When the baseball and football seasons were on, I still had my chores to do at home, but I would get up early and do many of them so that I could stay after school and practice with the teams. I still had to work some more when I got home at night, but I didn't mind it. I was enjoying life. I actually thought I might be good enough to make the major leagues in baseball.

When I graduated from high school I took a job with Eastern Airlines. Then when I got an offer from Western Electric to work for them so that I could play for their fast-pitch softball team, I took it. But I was anxious to complete my military obligation as quickly as possible, so I enlisted in the U.S. Army.

The day I left home for boot camp at Fort Jackson, South Carolina began a very dark period of my life. I somehow seemed to have left Jesus at home in Austell, and before long I was so deeply involved in sin that no one would have known that I had ever been a Christian. Like a dog, I had returned to the vomit of my former life. Like a sow, I had returned to the wallow.

Even now, after so many years, this period in my life is not easy for me to understand or explain. All I can say is that it happened. Perhaps it was the fact that I had led a fairly sheltered life until then and knew little of the outside world. Perhaps it was being out from under the firm hand of my Christian parents and grandparents for the first time. Perhaps it was the atmosphere of temptation and easy sin that existed around the military bases. Whatever the case, I quickly fell, I fell hard, and I showed no signs of getting up any time soon.

Like so many young Christians who get away from the Lord, I no doubt felt that I could just taste sin, just try it once or twice, and not get caught in its web. If so, I had greatly underestimated its power, and I was soon to learn that sin has a way of holding on to those who fall into its trap.

Once I was caught up in sin, there seemed to be no way out. It was not that I had forgotten God or my commitment to Him. I didn't hate God in any way, and I fully intended to serve Him ... someday. But the sin in my life made me feel unworthy to approach him. No one ever told me how easy God could deal with sin and how quickly He would receive me back and restore me. The shame of turning from Him kept me from even calling on His name, so there was no escape from my predicament.

I have also come to the conclusion, concerning this period in my life, that if I had been baptized in the Holy Ghost, I could have had power to resist sin. This is one of the reasons it bothers me that the truths of the Spirit-filled life are not being preached and received in some circles.

I was able to play baseball and football in the Army, so my time in the military passed quickly, but my spiritual life remained a shipwreck, and I didn't know what to do about it.

After I got out of the Army, I went back to work for Western Electric and continued to play ball for them, still hoping to make it into the big leagues. I loved the sport.

While I was working at Western Electric I met a lovely lady and fell in love with her. Her name was Mary Faulkner, and she was a fine Baptist believer. Even though I was not living for the Lord, I knew what I wanted in a wife, and soon I had convinced Mary to be my life's partner. I fully intended to get back into church, to clean up my life and to do the right thing. After we were married, however, nothing changed much. I attended church only sporadically. Church made me uncomfortable, and I increasingly found any excuse at all to avoid it. A year after we were married our daughter Robyn was born.

I enjoyed my work at Western Electric, but my hope for the big leagues seemed to be fading, and I learned that the Atlanta Police Department was looking for some new recruits. The pay was good and, as a military man, it seemed that I would have a leg up on the job, so I applied.

I was so sure that I would be accepted into the force that I resigned my job at Western Electric, and when my entrance into the force was delayed for a time, I had to go to work selling insurance. Our second child was on the way, so I had several mouths to feed. The very night that I was inducted into the Atlanta Police Department, another member was added to our family when our son Jim was born.

I liked police work and seemed to have an aptitude for it, so I moved quickly up the ladder, arriving eventually at the office of Police Lieutenant of Detectives assigned to Intelligence for the department. Things seemed to be going well for me, career wise, but spiritually they had not improved. One excuse led to another, one delay led to another, and the years passed without my getting back to God. This, and a very heavy work schedule began to put pressure on our marriage.

Mary was a great wife and mother, and I loved her, and we had two great kids, and I loved them too, but I was being pulled in too many directions at the moment. The demands of my job and my insistence on carrying on a night life with the boys at the department left me too little time for my family. Mary took the children to church regularly, but I had somehow become too busy for God as well.

The years flew quickly by, and suddenly I was thirty-two years old, and no one around me would have known that I had ever been a Christian. What a sad commentary! I was trapped in a miserable existence, not happy with my new life and not able to return to the old. God was about to intervene on my behalf, and he would do it through a great tragedy.

CHAPTER

FOUR

"IN MY TROUBLES, I CRIED TO THE LORD"

In my trouble I cried to the LORD, And He answered me.   Psalm 120:1

I SUPPOSE THAT EACH OF US CAN POINT TO A TIME IN OUR lives that we consider to have been the worst of times for us personally. Mine came when I was thirty-two years old and my daddy died.

When Daddy finally came home from the war, he had contracted a rare and debilitating blood disease and would have to be hospitalized off and on for the rest of his life. Mama did the best she could without his help, and she invested her whole life into me and my younger brother Bill. Life was not easy for her without a husband or for us without a father.

As sick as he was, it took my father twenty-two years to die. He finally breathed his last in the Veteran's Hospital in Decatur, Georgia. The last thing he said to me was, "Don't worry about me, son, I'm safe in the arms of Jesus!" Then he reached out, took Jesus by the hand and went home to glory. That was a dark day in my life, for he was my hero.

Our family doctor came to the funeral home to pay his respects and, standing by the casket, he gave me some more shocking news. I should be ready, he warned, for another funeral within thirty days. Mama had recently been diagnosed with terminal cancer, and her health was going downhill fast. My heart was torn. My parents had been everything to me, and now I was losing them both — on top of all my other problems.

Then something very unusual happened to me. Since I had grown up in a traditional church, I had never been taught anything about the Holy Spirit and His love for us. I didn't recognize that it was Him when I heard a voice saying to me, "Pray, and your mother will live." I only knew that I had to pray for Mama's life.

After Daddy's funeral, I got in the habit of going to the cemetery and sitting on the wall next to his grave to think. I was there the very next day after he was buried, and I decided to begin talking to God again and praying for my mother. I couldn't bear to lose her too.

"Lord," I prayed, "if You will heal my mother and extend her life with us, I will give you the rest of my life." It pained me to think that my parents would both leave while I was in such a wretched spiritual condition. "God," I prayed, "please let my mother see that her Christian example and the years of reading the Bible to my brother and me were not in vain. I will use all that she has taught me to serve You." And I meant it.

Mama totally recovered and lived for twenty-one more years. God was faithful to His promise, although I was not immediately as faithful to mine. I tried to give my all to God, but something was seriously lacking in my life. I would later learn that it was the power of the Holy Spirit that I needed.

I had not forgotten my promise to God, and I felt very convicted for not keeping it. He had kept His part of the bargain, and it was clearly my turn. I decided that I just had to make another effort to serve Him. I started going to church with my wife and children, worked with the youth, taught Sunday School and even became a deacon. It still wasn't enough. I somehow knew that God was calling me to more.

One Sunday morning I could not stand still during the altar call. I heard that voice again, and I ran down the aisle and told our pastor that I felt God was calling me to full-time ministry. His reply was discouraging: "You don't want to do that, son. Stay with the police department. You'll be much better off there."

That pastor didn't know much about the work of the Holy Spirit either, so he couldn't help me, and I didn't know anyone else who could. The opportunity was lost for the moment, and before long I had fallen back into my old routine. I did find things I could do for the Lord, but many more years went by without my fulfilling the call I felt on my life.

I knew what I had promised God, and I was sure now that it had been His voice telling me to pray for Mama and leading me down the aisle that Sunday morning to surrender my all to serve Him. I just wasn't sure what I should do next. How could I answer God's call? When the solution came, it would be in a most unexpected way.

Chapter

Five

"You Will Receive Power"

*You will receive power when the Holy Spirit
has come upon you.* Acts 1:8

I TOOK ANY OPPORTUNITY THAT CAME MY WAY TO PREACH,
even preaching a few revival meetings, but still my
desire to do something meaningful for God continued to grow. When I accepted an offer of some extra
hours doing security on Friday nights for a local
hotel, I came face to face with some very peculiar
people.

My shift ended at eight each Saturday morning,
and just before I got off work I would notice hundreds of people going into the ballroom where many
tables had been set up. I inquired and learned that

it was a breakfast meeting for a Christian group calling itself the Full Gospel Business Men's Fellowship International, whatever that was.

The FGBMFI meeting began at 7:00 a.m., so I stood near the door several Saturdays and listened to them a little. Those people were so excited about what the Holy Spirit was going to do for them that day. It interested me to hear people speaking of the Holy Spirit and His work, especially because my wife had had an encounter with the Holy Spirit not long before.

We had gone to hear a friend of mine preach. When it came time for the altar call he said, "If you would like to receive the baptism in the Holy Spirit, go to the back of the chapel, and someone will pray with you."

Before I could move, Mary turned to me and said, "I'll be back in a few minutes." When she came back, she was glowing all over and very excited. She kept saying, "I got it! I got it!"

"What did you get?" I asked.

"I got the baptism in the Holy Spirit," she replied.

This experience had changed Mary so much that now I wanted it too.

One Saturday morning as I stood outside the door to the ballroom, some people I knew came in. One of the men in the group invited me to sit with them at their table. I knew this man would not be involved

in anything that was not real. He was a very dignified person and was successful in the company he
worked for. I decided to take them up on their invitation and to join them when my shift ended.

It was a miracle that this other man was in that
meeting. He had not yet been baptized in the Holy
Spirit and was rather skeptical of the experience.
Like us, he had been taught that you get all there is
to the Holy Spirit when you get saved. What we had
not been taught was that the Holy Spirit does not
necessarily get all of us at salvation, and until He
does, we are walking in our own strength and not
in God's power.

When the altar call was given that morning, many
people went forward to receive the baptism in the
Holy Spirit. My friend and I stayed at the table ...
that is until his wife came back and urged us to go
forward for prayer. We finally agreed, but we said,
"We'll go, but we're not going to fall down." We
had seen many of those who went forward fall to
the floor, what the people there called "being slain
in the Spirit," and we had no intention of joining
them in something so foolish.

When we got up to the front, two men got behind
us to catch us when we fell. We told them we didn't
need their help because we were not going to fall
down. We had just come to pray. They said they
would stand by just in case we needed them.

Just then, Lynwood Maddox, a local attorney, walked up to my friend, laid his hands on his head and said, "In the name of Jesus, receive the baptism in the Holy Spirit!" My friend went down like a wet noodle onto his back and began to speak in tongues.

Next Lynwood laid hands on me. Within a split second I was flat on my back, and I was speaking in tongues too. I wasn't sure what was happening, but I felt like I had just laid down on a Florida beach and was soaking up a very hot sun, while ocean waves kept rolling over me. I felt hot inside. It was wonderful!

After a little while, I opened my eyes and looked over at my friend lying on the ballroom floor beside me. He looked at me, and that very dignified businessman and I burst out in laughter like I had never experienced before. We had it, the baptism of the Holy Spirit, and it totally changed our lives.

Now, instead of God being way off somewhere, just waiting for me to mess up so He could give me a whipping, He was in me, loving me and causing me to love everybody else. This was real, and I was enjoying it immensely.

I had heard of this experience of course, but I had always been taught that it had passed away with the apostles. Well, now I knew that couldn't be true, because I had it, and I knew that God wasn't about to take it away from me, just after He had given it to me. And it felt so good that I really couldn't be concerned about what others thought about it.

I still had a lot to learn, but I was on my way. I began to wonder: *Is it possible that since God didn't take away the baptism in the Holy Spirit, He also didn't take away the fruits and the gifts of the Spirit?* I was about to find out.

Chapter

Six

"These Signs Will Accompany
Those Who Have Believed"

These signs will accompany those who have believed: in My name they will cast out demons, they will speak with new tongues; they will pick up serpents, and if they drink any deadly poison, it will not hurt them; they will lay hands on the sick, and they will recover.

Mark 16:17-18

AFTER I WAS BAPTIZED IN THE HOLY SPIRIT, THE WORD of God became alive for me, and I began to believe Him for the complete fulfillment of it. He had said that it would *"not return ... void,"* that it would ac-

complish what He pleased and prosper or have success in its intent (Isaiah 55:11, KJV). I began to believe
it all, and to believe that it was for every Christian. I
was sure that God wanted signs to *"accompany those
who have believed,"* and I was about to get tested on
it.

Mary and I were in her hometown, Fitzgerald,
Georgia, at a local swimming pool one day, when I
noticed for the first time a very ugly-looking mole
on my arm. It certainly looked like it could be ma-
lignant.

After I showed the mole to Mary, I laid my hand
on it and told Jesus that I believed that by His stripes
I was healed. I was just saying what He had said in
His Word:

> *By whose [Christ's] stripes ye were healed.*
> 1 Peter 2:24, KJV

When I said that, the mole immediately disappeared.

Not long after that incident a friend called me in
great pain from a kidney stone and asked me if I
could come over and anoint him with oil and pray
for him. He had been suffering with this stone for
several days, and it was growing unbearable. I got
in the car and left immediately for his house.

When I got to the man's house, I realized that I

didn't have any oil, and he had specifically asked me to anoint him with oil, so before I went inside, I lifted the hood of my car and got some motor oil off the dipstick. I anointed my friend with the motor oil, prayed over him and went back home. Later that day he called to say that just after I had left he passed the kidney stone.

These two events proved to me that the power of the Holy Spirit was very real, and I began to read everything I could get my hands on about this. I wanted to know how the Spirit worked. Jack Taylor, who now happens to be a good friend of mine, had written several such books, and I devoured them in rapid order.

I didn't just accept everything the man had to say. As I read, I carefully checked each part of his teaching with God's Word, and I came to the conclusion that what he was saying was totally in keeping with the sacred Scriptures. Since he was a Baptist, this was all the more reason to trust his writings.

It wasn't long before I discovered that not every Baptist pastor was willing to be as open minded on this subject as I was and that many did not accept the teachings I was receiving as part of God's truth. How sad that was for me! I have never understood why anyone would put tradition above the truth. Jesus clearly taught that tradition makes the Word of God *"of none effect"* (Mark 7:13, KJV).

It seemed terrible to me that the pastors and teachers in the churches I had attended — first in childhood and then later in life — had never told me it was alright for me to believe and practice all the Word of God. I forgave them, but I still found it hard to understand.

It also troubled me that we had never been taught that the Kingdom of God was at hand and, in fact, in us. I had come to know this was true because He was living in me and manifesting Himself through me daily.

How great it was to experience the truths of the Scriptures:

> *Greater is He who is in you than he who is in the world.*   1 John 4:4

> *We are more than conquerors through him that loved us.*   Romans 8:37, KJV

I was enjoying my new-found power and was not about to back up for anyone or anything. I wanted more, and the pressure on my spirit to give myself fully to God's work was building. If it was wonderful to serve God as a layperson, it must be even more wonderful to serve Him fully. But how should I go about that?

Chapter

Seven

"It Shall Not Approach You"

A thousand may fall at your side And ten thousand at your right hand, But it shall not approach you. Psalm 91:7

GOD NEVER FORGETS OUR PROMISES, AND HE NEVER GIVES up on us. I was to learn these lessons the hard way. A series of tragic events was about to bring me to a place in my life that I could no longer say no to God.

My job had always been dangerous, but it suddenly became very dangerous. We had three major riots and many less serious disturbances in Atlanta, and I, unfortunately, found myself right in the middle of it all. In the coming days I was on the receiving end of gunfire, rocks, bricks and other missiles. Firebombs exploded on my police car. Twice the car was totally destroyed, although I was spared. God's promise of protection was working for me, but I was beginning to wonder if He was trying to get my attention.

God was with my brother Bill during those days as well, especially so the evening he was hit by a truck while on his way to a call. Bill was badly injured and was laid up for quite a while, but he eventually fully recovered.

One day, when I was riding with another detective, a man pulled his car in front of ours and stopped, got out and came around to my side of the patrol car. I thought he just wanted to ask us for directions, so I didn't even notice when he pulled a forty-five automatic pistol out of his belt. I did notice when he emptied the clip directly into my chest from three feet away.

My partner got on the radio and shouted, "Send an ambulance! The lieutenant has been shot!" I looked down at my chest, and was surprised to find that there were no bullet holes and no blood, and I had no pain. Somehow he had missed me at close range.

The shooter ran into a house and barricaded himself inside. In time, we were able to get the man out without hurting him or ourselves, but we were shaken by the whole affair. When we examined the squad car, we discovered that every bullet he had fired had gone into the car seat directly behind my back. How I wasn't hit we could never figure out. God had shown me again that He was with me, He had not given up on me, and He had a plan to bring me into a place of fulfilling my promise to serve Him completely.

By now I was serving as associate pastor of a church. I had organized a youth ministry I called Teens Set Free based on the promise of Jesus that the truth will set us free. At one time we had up to six hundred young people participating in that outreach. I had also conducted some youth revivals. But I had just turned forty, and I sensed that my time to serve the Lord more fully was getting closer. In fact, I sensed that it was now or never.

This series of events caused me to pray seriously. I said, "Lord, I'm ready when You are. Just let me know that I am walking in Your will, and I will do anything, go anywhere and serve You in any way You choose." Still, I did not act on it.

I was the day-watch Lieutenant in one of our zones in the City of Atlanta when one Wednesday morning a veteran police officer came into my office and asked me, "Lieutenant, is God still calling you to be a full-time pastor?"

I chose to keep the turmoil of my inner feelings to myself for the moment. "Yes, He is," I told him, "and

I'm going to do that just as soon as I retire from the Police Department." I had in so many years with the force that it just seemed reasonable to wait now until retirement to make any move. At least that is what I was telling anyone who asked.

"I'm not waiting," he told me. "I'm officially retiring as of this Friday. We never know what may happen. We may not even make it through the day. Remember what Jesus told the rich young ruler, that his life could very well end that day."

I respected what he said, and I simply answered, "Well, I'm praying about that."

"I'll be praying with you," he said, and he went out on a call.

After I got all the men out into the field, I gathered the night reports together and got in my car to take them to headquarters. I was about halfway there when I heard a Signal 63 coming in over the radio. This meant that an officer was in trouble and needed help. I recognized the address being given. It was an address from which we had been requested to transport a young man to the psychiatric ward of a local hospital. The officer who had gone to carry out that request was the man who had been in my office just minutes before and had spoken to me of the shortness of time.

I turned on my blue light and siren, stepped on the gas and went as fast as I could toward that part of town. While I was on my way, another call came over the radio advising me to proceed with caution because several shots had been fired, and an ambulance had been dispatched.

When I arrived at the scene, I saw the officer's car parked in the driveway, but he was nowhere to be seen. I got out of my car quickly and ran into the house. There I found a man lying on the living room floor. He had been shot. I checked his pulse and found that he was dead.

I moved toward the rear of the house and saw a woman lying on the floor. She was also dead.

I tried to open a door that seemed to lead to one of the bedrooms, but there was something heavy against the door, preventing me from opening it. I shoved the door, and when I was finally able to get it open enough to squeeze through, there I found the officer who had just moments before warned me to listen to God because we might not make it through the day. He was lying on the floor up against the door, and he was mortally wounded. I took my friend in my arms, and when I did, he looked into my eyes and whispered his last words on this Earth, "I told you so, Lieutenant." Just that quickly, he was gone into eternity.

By this time, many other police cars and ambulances had arrived. I grabbed a shotgun out of my car and went toward the woods where a neighbor said the shooter had run after killing his own mother and father and my friend, the thirty-five-year veteran police officer.

I caught sight of the boy hiding behind a tree, just as he leaned out with a pistol pointed toward me. I could have blown him away in that moment, but, suddenly the love of God welled up in me for him, and I was not able to pull the trigger. God loved that boy, and He was loving him through me.

I laid the shotgun down and started moving slowly toward him. "Either kill me or give me the gun," I said to him, and for a moment it appeared that it could have gone either way. In the end, he dropped the gun on the ground and surrendered.

As soon as everything was settled at the crime scene, I went directly to my chief's office and resigned. I said, "Chief, I have to do what God wants me to do, and I have to do it now!"

"I understand," he said. "What are your plans?"

"I have none," I replied, "but I will follow God's plans from now on. God bless you, I will always pray for you."

"Thanks," the Chief replied, his eyes filled with tears.

I went right home and told Mary that we were in the ministry. I didn't know where we were to serve, but I was sure that God did know.

Chapter

Eight

"I Will Build My Church"

I will build My church; and the gates of Hades will not overpower it.   Matthew 16:18

ALMOST IMMEDIATELY I GOT A CALL FROM A CHURCH IN Savannah, Georgia, inviting me to come and preach and be interviewed to be their pastor. I had sent a resume some time before to the Baptist Mission Board, and they had forwarded it, along with many other resumes, to churches that were looking for pastors. The men in charge of the selection process in Savannah told me they had gone through the resumes of many prospective pastors, but they felt God kept bringing them back to me. I was excited, but the kids didn't seem to like the idea of moving.

Robyn was in her senior year in high school, and moving seemed like a traumatic idea to her, and Jim was very happy with his school as well. Still, the entire family agreed to go with me to at least see the place.

I prayed all the way down to Savannah, "Lord, if this is the church you want me to pastor, show me through my wife and kids. Let us all be in agreement about this thing."

When we got to Savannah, the odor of a local paper mill was enough to make me want to turn around and go back home. I thought to myself, *Don't worry, it would take a real miracle for all of us, especially Robyn and Jim, to be in agreement to stay here.* Anyway, the church would have to hear me preach, and then I would have to be interviewed personally. It was a long process. Surely they would not choose me.

When we got to the church, I was even more certain that my family would not like the place. The church was located in the country and had a wild-life-protected swamp behind it. Between the pastor's house and the swamp was the church cemetery. *Forget it,* I thought, *there's no way they will want to live here.*

After I had preached that morning, someone showed us around the property. While Mary and I were looking at the parsonage, we suddenly heard

Robyn and Jim arguing in a back bedroom. When I asked them what the fuss was all about, Jim said, "I want this to be my room, and Robyn said she gets first choice because she's the oldest, and she wants this room." God was working in my children.

On the way home, Mary and the children agreed that they wanted to move to Savannah, but I was still doubtful that the church would actually call me. Not long after we got home, however, the Chairman of Deacons called me to say that the church had voted to extend the call for me to be their pastor. We sold our home in Austell, Georgia and moved to Savannah.

Not long after we got to Savannah, one of the women attending our Wednesday morning Bible study was praying. She said, "Lord, save my husband — no matter what You have to do." After the Bible study I went back to the house, and there was a phone call waiting for me. That lady's husband had suffered a massive heart attack and was on his way to the hospital. I met them there and learned that the prognosis for his recovery was not good.

That night we were praying for him in the church, and as we asked God to heal him, I saw in my spirit a human heart that was almost black, and it had a black veil draped over it. When we prayed the words *"by His stripes, we are healed,"* the veil lifted, and the heart turned red and perfectly healthy.

I immediately went to the hospital to tell the family what God had shown me. As I came down the hall to the Coronary Care Unit, I met the man walking down the hall toward me completely dressed. He said that about the time we were praying, all the pain and discomfort had left him, and he knew that he was healed. He accepted Jesus Christ as his Savior right then and there. The last time I knew that man was still healed.

That single miracle brought revival to the church, and within a few weeks of our having taken the church, the sanctuary was full for every service. There was not one empty seat in the place. We even had people standing in the foyer throughout the services.

We knew that we were in revival when the pastor of the largest church in Savannah called and asked how we were doing it. I told him that all I knew was that the Holy Spirit was alive and well in our church, and that He was doing it all, not me, and certainly not any program that we had put into place. We baptized more people that year than any other church in our area.

After we were in Savannah for two years, one of the wealthy members of the church called me one day and said that if we would build a larger sanctuary she would pay for it. I called the deacons together and told them what the woman had said, but they concluded that if we built another sanctuary it might hide the cemetery, and they could not agree to that. I sensed, right then and there, that my time was about finished in Savannah. When we are afraid to hide the dead in order to bring life into the community, what can God do for us?

Soon after that, God spoke to another pulpit committee to invite me to preach, this time in Austell, Georgia, the very town I had grown up in. It wasn't long before I was called back to pastor one of the largest churches in the area. The only problem was that the church had recently split, there were now only about seventy people left, and they had a large debt to pay down.

By then, however, I knew that the Lord could build up His Church very quickly, and I was not concerned by these apparent negatives. They wouldn't hinder God.

Chapter

Nine

"Do Not Quench the Spirit"

Do not quench the Spirit.

1 Thessalonians 5:19

IT WAS NOT UNTIL I GOT BACK TO AUSTELL THAT I LEARNED the reason that the church I had taken split. It was because the pastor had gone to Titusville, Florida, to hear a group of Spirit-filled men: Peter Lord, Manley Beasley and Jack Taylor. While he was in that meeting, the Holy Spirit hit him, and he came home on fire for Jesus. I had never realized that you could be in trouble as a pastor with your people for getting on fire for Jesus.

There was more to it than that, of course. He had

been baptized in the Holy Spirit and spoken in tongues, and he was intent on opening his people up to the power-filled life by preaching and teaching these truths. This had ruffled a lot of feathers.

At the first deacons' meeting held after I took the church, I was told that I had a free hand as pastor, but that I could not go to Titusville, Florida or get involved with any of "that Holy Spirit stuff." I made the serious mistake of not speaking up immediately. I chose, instead, not to say anything right then about my experience. Maybe God could use me to open them up — if I just kept quiet and let Him do it.

The former pastor and the members who had left with him were meeting in a local high school. They had bought some land several miles away, and I learned that they intended to build a Spirit-filled Baptist church there. They had raised enough money in a single service to pay off the land and put up a new building. When I walked into the local Christian book store one day, several of them were there, and they began to shout and laugh. "They ran off one Holy Ghost pastor," they said, "and then they turned around and called another one in his place." We all agreed that God had a wonderful sense of humor.

Through a lot of hard work and prayer, God brought a revival of souls to my new assignment. We consistently led our association in water baptisms, our sanctuary was filled in every service, and we paid off every debt the congregation owed.

We did not see many actual miracles in that place, however, because the Holy Spirit was not allowed to do His work. In spite of that hindrance, we saw hundreds of people saved and others rededicated and back into church. God did as much as men would allow Him to do. He met us in our level of faith, but we could not go beyond it.

After I had been in that setting for several years, I began to automatically put the Holy Spirit on the back burner, and when we insist on ruling instead of allowing Him to rule, He cannot do His full work. For the next two and a half years I was a miserable man.

The church was treating me well in every way, but I was not happy because I was not free to allow the manifestations of the Holy Spirit to work in my ministry. I eventually sensed that trouble was coming, and I did not want to be the cause of another split in the church, so I was feeling that I needed to make a change.

One day, when I was visiting the hospital, a lady from a Spirit-filled church came up to me and told me that her church had been praying for me. The Lord told them that I was going to leave my church and go to a church that seemed impossible to resurrect. I was not to fear, she said, because God was in charge, and He would use the situation to do great things: miracles, signs and wonders. She told me that I would have more people saved than in any of the churches I had pastored until then.

I wasn't sure at first what to make of all this, but as I prayed, the Holy Spirit spoke to me to listen to this woman because she was conveying to me what He had told her. I thanked the lady and left.

Not long after this, Robyn became seriously ill and had to be hospitalized. Despite many tests, our doctor could not discover what her problem was. She grew worse every day and finally was so sick that she had to be moved to the Intensive Care Unit. Eight specialists were called in to see if her life could be saved.

One day the doctor came into the ICU Waiting Room and told me that Robyn was in immediate danger of dying. Her blood platelet count had dropped to a very dangerous level. The man was a personal friend, as well as our doctor, and he was also a Christian. I told him that Mary and I were going home to pray.

When we got home, we took Robyn's Bible, laid our hands on it and began to pray. We somehow felt that Robyn's sickness was God's way of dealing with us. We promised Him, in that moment, that if He would heal Robyn we would go anywhere and do anything for Him — even if He wanted us to preach on street corners.

We returned to the hospital, and our doctor met us to report that a miracle was in the making. Robyn's platelet count had started rising fast. The next day it was normal, and the following day she was able to go home, completely healed.

We were grateful to God for having touched our daughter, and we didn't forget our promise to Him. I resigned as pastor of the church the next week, and we suddenly had no place to go and no family income.

To support the family, I took a temporary job working security for a friend of mine, and then I started selling insurance, all the while preaching every opportunity I got. I did well selling insurance, making more money than I had ever made in my life, but I knew that this was not my future. I was waiting patiently for the Lord to show us His plan. At the same time, I was anxious to see where He would be leading us next. It didn't take long to find out.

Chapter

Ten

"The Despised God Has Chosen"

The base things of the world and the despised God has chosen, the things that are not, so that He may nullify the things that are.

1 Corinthians 1:28

AT ONE POINT, I HAD BEGUN TO THINK THAT I HAD PROBABLY finished my work as a pastor and that I was about to embark on a new era of ministry — as an evangelist. This was not a totally new ministry to me. I had preached some revivals while I was still on the police force in Atlanta, the ministry of evangelism had always appealed to me, and I had always seen good results for my efforts, many people saved. I had the idea of sending out a letter to churches and lining up a series of revival meetings. I was planning to order new calling cards and letterheads with my title changed to evangelist. Then one day I got a phone call from a church on Old Alabama Road in Austell.

The caller said, "I'm the only deacon left at Friendship Baptist Church. As a matter of fact, we have only twelve people left here. We have no one to help us, and we just heard that you left your church. Would you be willing to come and help us until we can at least get rid of our property and dissolve the congregation?"

Friendship Baptist was a church that Mary and I had passed many times as we were going to and from services in other churches. We had known that they were in trouble when we sometimes saw no more than two or three cars there during service times. I always had a strange feeling about the church, however, and had remarked to Mary that God seemed to be showing me something about it. He seemed to be saying to me, "There lies a sleeping giant!"

Suddenly this all made sense to me, and I knew that God wanted me to accept this invitation and pastor the church. I wasn't about to make the same mistake again, though, and I told the deacon who called me that I would be glad to help them, but that they needed to know that I was baptized in the Holy Spirit and spoke in tongues. Never again would I keep silent about this experience. Since the Holy Spirit gives us power, I was determined to lead as many people as I could into the experience.

The deacon quickly responded, "Good, that's what we need." He later told me that he hadn't been able to imagine how anything could possibly hurt the church at that point more than it was already hurting. It was *gone* as far as he was concerned.

But God had other ideas. No church is dead when the Holy Ghost is allowed to take charge.

Because of the low attendance at their services, the remaining deacons of Friendship Baptist had closed the main sanctuary of the church and were having their meetings in a basement-type building in back. The church had begun in that "back building," and they were now back to their beginnings. They had always intended to put a second story on this building, but they had never needed it. I held my first service in that "back building" on a Wednesday night, and my first sermon was on the power of God enabling us to do His work.

All twelve members were present that night, and they were loving my message ... until I began to tell them about my experience of being baptized in the Holy Ghost and speaking in tongues. After that night, half of the congregation never came back. We were down to six members. So much for the sleeping giant.

But we were not dead in any sense of the word. As the Holy Spirit took over our services and began to manifest Himself, we quickly began to grow in number, and it wasn't long before we had outgrown the "back building" and were back in the main sanctuary, where we could seat about two hundred and fifty people.

We began supplementing our standard hymns with praise and worship music, and as we worshiped, the anointing would fill the church. During our altar calls, people were being saved, healed, delivered and baptized in the Holy Spirit. For the next sixteen years, we were to lead the churches in our area in salvations, baptisms, healings and deliverances — not to mention the signs and wonders and miracles that God was doing in every service.

One lady came to the church in the midst of a heart attack. Her husband had been rushing her to the hospital and, as they neared the church, the Holy Spirit directed them to stop and come in for prayer. When we prayed for that woman, Holy Ghost power fell on her, and she was immediately healed.

Another lady who came forward had hands that were drawn closed from acute arthritis. God's healing power fell on her, and she stood there weeping with joy as we all watched her fingers straighten out. It sounded like sticks breaking, as the power of God pulled the arthritis loose and healed her. She never had problems with arthritis again.

Word spread that hundreds of salvations and healings were taking place at Friendship Baptist Church, and people drove from many miles around to experience God. Revival had hit and brought God's Holy Spirit life to our church.

We were growing so quickly that we decided to buy more land. We bought five more acres, believing that God would help us pay it off within seven years. Instead, we paid it off in seven months.

The current sanctuary was filling up quickly because Heaven was falling on every service, and amazing things were happening. I sensed that we were going to need more room, more quickly than we had anticipated, so one day I walked over to the new property, broke some ground by faith and claimed a new and larger sanctuary.

Not everyone was happy with what was happening in the church. Pastors from other churches began to severely criticize us, sometimes from the pulpit. One pastor even said that what we were experiencing was "of the devil." (May God forgive him.) Another pastor told me that he never wanted this to happen in his church. I asked him if he was preaching about the Holy Spirit and allowing Him to work. He said that he didn't believe in it. I told him not to worry about it happening in his church, that it came only to those who believed.

Eventually two Baptist pastors were sent to examine my theology. They told me that what I was teaching was not accepted in the Baptist church. I reached for my Bible, laid it on the desk in front of them and welcomed them to tear out everything that Baptists were not supposed to be preaching. I would only preach and teach what was left I told them.

I went on to tell them, however, that when we all stood before God, I would not be afraid to tell Him that I had taught, preached and practiced God's Word, and I asked them if they could face Him in the same way.

They declined to tear any pages out of my Bible, got up and left. That year some of the leadership in our area tried to stir up other pastors and leaders against me, but, some good men of God stood up for us and said, "Leave him alone, lest you be found fighting against God and blaspheming the Holy Ghost!" Thank God for such men.

I went to see our association's missionary and told him about what I was experiencing. He prayed with me and told me that if I followed God I could never go wrong. I was grateful to God for him, too.

Criticism didn't seem to hinder God. Miraculous healings and deliverances continued to take place at Friendship Baptist. Hundreds were saved, and we totally outgrew the sanctuary. By faith we broke ground on our new property and began to build a new sanctuary. We hoped to have two-thirds of the new building for growth, but it, too, would fill up much faster than we expected.

Chapter

Eleven

"Enlarge the Place of Your Tent"

Enlarge the place of your tent; Stretch out the curtains of your dwellings, spare not; Lengthen your cords And strengthen your pegs. For you will spread abroad to the right and to the left. And your descendants will possess nations And will resettle the desolate cities. Isaiah 54:2-3

WHAT GOD DID OVER TIME IN OUR OWN FAMILY IS A STORY in itself, and the response of our family members made possible much of the expansion we did over the coming years.

As the work in Austell continued to grow, I desperately needed help, and God gave me that help in the form of my brother Bill. Bill had been filled with the Spirit long before I had, and he and his wife Reba had been members of an Assembly of God Church. In 1990, after he retired from the police force, he became my associate pastor, and he has been very faithful to the church ever since.

Bill and I, with one other couple, started a church in Tennessee. At first we just joined that couple every Thursday in prayer for a Spirit-filled church for their town, but over time, God answered our prayers wonderfully. The last I heard that church was full in every service. They have about six hundred members, and are still growing.

My wife Mary has been a strong tower in my life from the beginning of our journey of faith, and has constantly encouraged me to move forward into new areas of faith. She has always been by my side in every decision I made. I could not have come this far without her by my side.

Eventually, we developed another congregation in Douglasville, in Paulding County, or should I say, another location? We are actually one congregation with two different locations. Having a location in Douglasville saved people from having to drive so far to find a Spirit-filled Baptist church.

It was, of course, impossible for me to pastor the two locations and do everything else I was doing. Jim had been away from the Lord for a few years during the late eighties, but Mary and I prayed earnestly and constantly for him, and in 1992 God brought him back to the church. By the time the Paulding County work was started, Jim had not only returned to the Lord, but had also consecrated his life to the ministry and become my associate. He took responsibility for the Paulding County work and preaches there regularly.

Both Jim and Bill are Spirit-filled faith preachers who present God's message of hope and salvation just as well as I do. Many baptisms in the Holy Spirit take place under their ministry as well as salvations, healings and deliverances. I am very proud of both of them and what God is doing in their ministries. We have Holy Ghost fire falling at both locations in every service.

Our daughter Robyn has also blessed our ministry immeasurably. She is in charge of our praise and worship ministry, and every visitor tells me that they consider her anointing for music to be second to none. She also has an anointing for the youth and meets with them every week. And she works faithfully in the church office and in any other way I need her to help in the ministry.

God was supplying our every need.

Even though we began feeding people from Friendship Baptist into other churches in an effort to see God move in those places (we have blessed at least sixteen other works in this way), God always replaced the ones we sent out with two new ones.

Our outreach was expanding in other ways, as well. In the early part of 1995, Pastor Eddie Rogers called me. He was the pastor of Sweet Spirit Baptist Church in Hiram, Georgia, and he wanted me to come and do a week of meetings with him to see if I could get his people to open up to the Holy Spirit. He had heard about the awesome things God was doing in our ministry, and he thought: *If they can have it, then I can too.* He was on the right track, but he just didn't know how to get started.

I asked him if he was sure he understood what we were all about. "Along with a move of God comes persecution," I warned.

He answered, "I understand, and I want it," so I went.

I opened my meeting with him on a Sunday, and went through that Friday. During those few days we saw many manifestations of the Spirit of God and felt His mighty presence with us at all times.

On one particular night, there were several Southern Baptist pastors and evangelists present. When I began to minister, Eddie came down first. He wanted me to lay hands on him. He went down in the Spirit and began to speak in tongues.

Others then lined up and wanted this blessing.

Pastor/Evangelist Keith Ellis, the favorite evangelist of many Baptist churches, came down to the altar, I laid hands on him, and he went down in the Spirit and began to speak in tongues.

A great big brother, a member of a worship team, whom we, interestingly enough, called Tiny (Tiny Schaus), hit the floor like a ton of bricks, and he too began to speak in other tongues.

These were just three of many who were blessed in those meetings and an indication of what God wanted to do with pastors and other Christian leaders. In all, more than one hundred and eighty Baptist pastors have come into this experience.

Although God has used us to bring many Baptists to this experience — both Southern Baptists and Independent Baptists as well — I have also seen many Methodists baptized in the Holy Ghost and many Catholics, Presbyterians and people from many other denominations, including some from the Pentecostal denominations who have never been baptized in the Holy Ghost.

I began to teach the people everywhere I went the danger of tradition and tried to open them to the Word of God. As they opened up, God began to work with them. In our area alone, I have ministered the Holy Spirit to sixteen Baptist pastors who are now flowing in these blessings.

Not all of those who were filled with the Spirit

stayed in the Baptist church. Some did, and some didn't, but they are all demonstrating God's power in their lives. This new experience has brought life to their ministries and their churches, and we are blessed in having a part in it.

As we took God's power out to others, He was making sure that we were amply blessed at home.

Chapter

Twelve

"God Was Performing

Extraordinary Miracles"

*God was performing extraordinary miracles by
the hands of Paul, so that handkerchiefs or
aprons were even carried from his body to the
sick, and the diseases left them and the evil spirits went out.* Acts 19:11-12

REVIVAL FIRES CONTINUED TO BURN AT FRIENDSHIP
Baptist Church. Some outstanding miracles that God
did during that period are typical of the great things
He was doing for us.

One day a lady who was a patient in the hospital
requested a visit from a chaplain and, since I serve
as a volunteer chaplain for the hospital, I was called
to visit her. Bill went with me that day.

Cancer had gotten into her bones, and even her spinal chord was deteriorated. She could die at any moment. As we talked with her, we learned that she was lost without Christ. I asked her if she believed that Jesus Christ was the Son of God and that He died on the cross for her sins and for her sicknesses. She said she did.

"Do you believe that God raised Him from the dead?" I asked.

She said that she did.

"Do you want Jesus to come into your heart, save your soul and heal your body?" I asked her.

"Yes," she answered.

She prayed, asking Jesus to come into her heart, to be her Savior and to be the Lord of her life. She asked Him to touch her and heal her body and fill her with the Holy Spirit. She was gloriously saved that day right there in her hospital bed. It would have been her death bed, but what she did that day turned her life around.

That Sunday the woman got her brother to take her in a wheelchair to our church. Four big men lifted her and the chair into the baptismal pool and we baptized her, wheelchair and all.

After that day, the sister came to church often in her wheelchair. Then one day we saw her come in the door with a walker. She made her way to the front and sat down. She had the most wonderful smile on her face. She was supposed to be dead long ago, but God had touched her, and she had hope for the future.

Then one day she came in the door, and she no longer had the walker. She was supporting herself with two waking sticks.

A week or two later, she came in the door with only one of the walking sticks for support. The miracle was happening.

One day, as I was crossing the church parking lot, going to the rear to get a cup of coffee before the evening service, I heard a car pull up and someone get out and close the door. My back was to the car, so I didn't see who it was. Then I heard someone shouting at the top of their voice, "Pastor! Pastor!"

I turned and saw this same woman, just as she took off running toward me. She had driven herself to church and now told me that she was totally healed. Tests showed that she was completely cancer free.

On another occasion I was called to the hospital by the family of our guitar player. He was in his late sixties at the time and had a serious heart condition. The family had been called in by the doctors and told to prepare for his funeral. Moments later, as I was on my way to the hospital, he was pronounced dead.

When I arrived, they told me what had happened, but I wanted to lay hands on the man and pray for him anyway. If Jesus could raise up Lazarus after he was dead already four days, surely He could raise this man up who had just died moments before. I laid my hands on the brother, anointed him with oil and prayed.

As I was finishing my prayer, he opened his eyes and said, "Thank God, you came, Brother Bob! I was already up in the ceiling looking down at my dead body. I heard and saw everything. I'm healed, now, thanks be to God and to your faith." That brother completely recovered and went on to live a productive life.

Another type of miracle was becoming common among us. Because we could not be everywhere at once, the Lord was leading us to use prayer cloths. We found that the Apostle Paul had done it in his day:

> *God was performing extraordinary miracles by the hands of Paul, so that handkerchiefs or aprons were even carried from his body to the sick, and the diseases left them and the evil spirits went out.*   Acts 19:11-12

When the anointing of God was present and operating in our services, we would pray over the cloths and then the members would take them out to the sick. Amazing miracles resulted, just as they had in Bible days.

Jack Raburn, one of my staff members, visited a man in the hospital. This man had terminal cancer and had been given only a few days to live. That very day he was to be released into the care of Hospice so that he could die in peace and dignity.

Jack took with him a prayer cloth from one of our services. He laid that prayer cloth on the chest of the sick man, and the anointing from the services began to flow into him. Within days he was well and at home.

One of the men of our church had a brother who had suffered a massive heart attack and wasn't given much hope for survival. He took one of the prayer cloths to his brother from the services, the anointing flowed into him, touched him, and he was restored.

One of our ladies had a sister with cancer, so she took one of the prayer cloths from the services to her. When she laid that prayer cloth on her sister, the anointing flowed into her, touched her, and she survived.

We have sent out prayer cloths all over the world. We give out hundreds of them during our services, and they really work. This anointing is so special that everywhere the glory goes, there is healing and salvation. God truly honors the preaching of the Good News of Jesus Christ with signs and wonders and miracles following.

That's what our Lord Jesus Christ can do! That's the kind of power the God I serve has! He declared to us in His Word that He took upon Himself our sicknesses and bore our infirmities, and by His stripes we are healed. We continued to believe it, and He continued to demonstrate it to us day by day.

Chapter

Thirteen

"To Make a Lamp Burn Continually"

You shall charge the sons of Israel, that they bring you clear oil of beaten olives for the light, to make a lamp burn continually.

Exodus 27:20

WHEN I HEARD ABOUT THE GREAT REVIVAL TAKING PLACE in Pensacola, Florida, at the Brownsville Assembly of God Church, I immediately wanted to go and experience it. If God was giving Pastor John Kilpatrick and Evangelist Steve Hill something new, I wanted it too. Bill went with me, and we got a front-row seat directly in the center, facing the pulpit. I always make it a point to get as close to the fire as I can. The closer I get to the altar, I reason, the more of the anointing I will feel and experience.

The service started with some very anointed music, and immediately I felt the presence of the Holy Spirit. Later, when John Kilpatrick and Steve Hill got up to the podium, I was nearly overcome with the demonstration of God's power.

They asked if any pastors needed prayer, and I stepped forward along with others. Steve Hill laid hands on me, and I hit the floor and skidded on my back up the aisle several feet. As I lay there, I heard God speak to me. He said, "Get up, the pastor wants to speak to you. He has a message for you."

I was thinking, *I don't even know this man, and why would he want to speak to me?* But when I opened my eyes, an usher was standing over me. He said that the pastor wanted me to come up on the podium because he had something he wanted to say to me.

I went up, and John Kilpatrick said to me, "You're a pastor who's hungry for more of God. God is going to shake your church, and when He is finished shaking it, you will experience a great revival."

I was stunned by all this, but great revival was what I wanted, and I didn't care what God had to do in order to give it to us.

Sure enough, when I went back to my church, God sent a great shaking. After He was through shaking everything that could be shaken, He told me that it was time to begin real revival.

I felt that I needed an outside speaker to take us

to the new level God was telling us about, so I went back to Pensacola and talked to John Kilpatrick and Steve Hill and asked if they could recommend someone who had the Brownsville anointing to come to my church for revival. They both pointed to a man in the congregation and said, "Ask the Chaplain."

The man they had pointed to, Carey Robertson, had indeed been a Navy chaplain. After he retired from the Navy, he pastored an Assembly of God church in Albany, Georgia. He resigned the church when he felt that God wanted him to go to Pensacola and be part of the Brownsville revival. I spoke with him and asked him to come and hold a revival for us. He told me he would pray about it and gave me his phone number.

I called the brother the next morning, and we arranged to meet to discuss his coming to Friendship Baptist for revival meetings. After hearing more about our church, he decided to come. I was very excited because God was breaking down denominational walls. This man was not a Baptist.

Our revival with Carey Robertson was glorious and continued for twenty-four weeks, until John Kilpatrick needed him and called him back to Brownsville. They were the most powerful meetings we had ever seen. Fifteen hundred people were saved, sixty-five hundred rededicated their lives to God and were baptized in the Holy Spirit, and more than twenty-five thousand people were ministered to altogether. It was during that great revival that the Lord gave us the name for our ministry, Revival Fires.

We had every type of miracle happen during those weeks of revival:

One lady came in one night with her husband and told an usher that our church sign was on fire. He went to look, and the sign was indeed glowing with the glory of God. That lady and her husband were both saved and baptized in the Holy Spirit. They had not even known that the revival was going on. They were just passing by when they saw the sign on fire. God certainly knows how to reach people.

Another lady came in and got saved in a very similar way. She said she was going down the highway and saw a spotlight coming from the sky. The light was so strange that she decided to follow it, to see what it was shining on and why. She made several turns as she followed the light and finally ended up at our church. The spotlight was focused directly on top of the sanctuary. The life of that lady was gloriously changed that night by a miracle of God.

During that twenty-four week revival, our people began doing another very unusual thing. We had placed a table at the altar in the sanctuary that we called a prayer table and people placed prayer requests there that we prayed over every day. Now people began putting others items there to be anointed: candy, gum and articles of clothing. When they later took these items from the prayer table and offered them to friends and family members who had proven difficult to witness to, those individuals would begin to weep, and would eventually come to the revival and be saved. Alcoholics, drug addicts, drug pushers, prostitutes, pimps and many other such hardened sinners were saved in this way.

The anointing was so strong in the church that people just passing by would turn in, park and come in to see what was going on. God touched them, saved them and delivered them right then and there.

Over the coming months and years, this anointing was to stay with us, and great miracles would be performed. We had, for instance, a little four-year-old girl with spina bifida brought to one of our services from Florida. She could not move her body from the waist down and, therefore, had never walked. We laid hands on that child, and the very next day she was running around. She came into the church, ran down the aisle, ran up on the podium and jumped off. She was totally and completely healed and has maintained her healing over time through the glory of God.

Two different women were told that their babies were dead in the womb and they would have to undergo abortions. We laid hands on them, and God brought life to the babies. Both babies were born normal and are alive and well today.

We had a baby girl who was born blind and deaf. I took that child in my arms, and as we all sang the old hymn "Amazing Grace," I lifted that child up to God and He healed her. Today she has 20/20 vision and perfect hearing.

I laid hands on a man who needed quintuple heart bypass surgery, and God healed him.

His son, thirty-one years old, who had an ileostomy, also came to the altar. He had a diseased kidney, and, for some reason, his bladder was shrunken. We felt the healing power of God come over him as we prayed. He went back to his doctor and was told that he could take the ileostomy bag off, that his kidney and bladder were normal. He still functions today without the bag.

Those who have never experienced these things may find all this difficult to believe. I would just say to them, "Stop by sometime, and see for yourself!"

It's not hard to have revival when the Holy Spirit is present. May every pastor and every church burn with desire for these same experiences.

For us, the life in the Spirit was getting better and better all the time.

Chapter

Fourteen

"Lengthen Your Cords"

Enlarge the place of your tent; Stretch out the
curtains of your dwellings, spare not; Lengthen
your cords And strengthen your pegs. For you
will spread abroad to the right and to the left.
And your descendants will possess nations And
will resettle the desolate cities. Isaiah 54:2-3

THE TWENTY-FOUR WEEK REVIVAL AT FRIENDSHIP WAS NOT
only a time of serious expansion at home. We also
began to reach out more into our community and
the world. We were lengthening our cords, strength-
ening our pegs and spreading abroad to the right
and to the left.

In the fall of 1998, Jim and I made a trip to Roma-
nia and Moldova. We separated so that we could

preach in several different places. He went to several villages to preach, while I went to several other villages to preach. God did awesome miracles in those days, and hundreds of people came to the Lord as a result of those meetings.

The people in those countries are so hungry for God, so starved for hope. Our message was hope in the Lord Jesus Christ, and we assured the people of Eastern Europe that Jesus could change their lives — and not only here on Earth. We told them of the ultimate hope, eternal life in Heaven. The response was utterly amazing. An eighteen-year-old girl had a withered arm. It had not developed normally from infancy. She came forward and asked, "Do you think God can heal my arm?"

"I know He can," I said to her. "Just lift up your arms and begin to praise the Lord." She lifted up the good arm, but the other one would not move. "Lift up the other one," I encouraged her.

"I can't," she said. "I've never been able to lift it. I can't even move it. It's frozen in this position."

"You *can* move it," I insisted, "in the name of Jesus, you *can* move it. You *can* lift it up."

I could see her muscles straining as she tried to raise up that arm. Then suddenly, something popped, and her arm began to move. In fact, it flew upward, and as it did, it began to grow to a normal size. When we had finished praying, that arm was exactly the same size as the other one.

She wept and praised the Lord. She had longed for that healing for eighteen years and it had now come, all because of the anointing of the Lord Jesus Christ and faith in Him. Jesus will always confirm His Word. He said that we would lay hands on the sick and they would recover.

While I was preaching in one of the churches, a man ran forward and asked to use the microphone. He said he had not been able to hear for years. He had come hoping against hope for a miracle. While I was preaching, his ears had popped, and now he could hear equally well out of both ears.

A lady who was blind came forward and said that her eyes had been opened, that scales had fallen from them and that she could see.

We saw such amazing miracles in those places, and I am convinced that it was because the people had no tradition to overcome. They were under communist rule for so many years and were denied the opportunity to publicly worship the Lord, to trust in Jesus as their Savior, to know His Word. Now they come by the hundreds and thousands to the feet of the Savior they have longed for so long. It is not difficult for them to experience a touch from Heaven.

Jim experienced the same amazing demonstration of God's power in his meetings. People were saved, healed and delivered, as the Spirit confirmed the Word he preached.

This trip confirmed to us that God is ready to move in any part of the world and for anyone who will do two things: (1) Be willing to let the Holy Spirit work as He wants to and (2) Be careful to give all the glory to God.

God had something much more powerful awaiting us, and it came in a most unexpected way.

Chapter

Fifteen

"The Knowledge of the Glory of the Lord"

For the earth will be filled
With the knowledge of the glory of the LORD,
As the waters cover the sea.

Habakkuk 2:14

SOMETIME IN LATE 1997 MY SECRETARY ATTENDED A meeting in another church in our area, and there she heard Ruth Ward Heflin minister. She was deeply impressed, for this anointed lady carried with her a weight of glory that few have experienced, and very unusual things happened in the service. The first time she saw me after this, my secretary gave me some phone numbers and told me that I needed to call Ruth Heflin and get her to come to our church.

I had no idea who Ruth Heflin was and hadn't yet read any of her books, so I politely received the telephone numbers, but did nothing. It was nearly a year later when the Lord spoke to me one Saturday morning as I was getting up and told me to call Ruth Heflin. If I would call her and get her to my church, the Lord said, He would use her to impart something new to us.

I called Sister Ruth at her home that day, but she wasn't in, so I left a message. I told her who I was, that the Lord had put on my mind to call her, that I wanted her to come and speak for us in the church and that the Lord said He had something He was going to do for us while she was with us in the church.

Ruth wasn't able to answer me for a week or two, but she finally called one Saturday. I fell in love with this gracious lady instantly, and she responded very favorably to my query. "How could I refuse a Baptist pastor with such a request?" she said.

"So you'll come?" I asked. "When can you come? We're anxious."

"Well," she said, "I know it's awfully short notice, but since I'm going to be in Atlanta later next week anyway, how about if I come for Tuesday and Wednesday of next week? We could do three services: Tuesday night, Wednesday morning and Wednesday night."

"That's fine," I told her, and we started announcing the meetings.

Our people got the news out very quickly, and a good crowd of people showed up at the church for Tuesday night. Even before Ruth began preaching, flecks of gold began appearing on her, on her clothing and on her face.

While she was preaching that night, she broke into song: "There's a wheel within the wheel, and it's turning in me." It was a song the Lord had given her some years before, and many of us gathered at the altar of the church and began dancing before the Lord. I was dancing with my wife and daughter, and while we danced Ruth laid her hands on me. I got drunk in the Spirit and fell down on the floor. Suddenly I was caught up to the throne room of God, for the first time in my life.

The Lord began to speak to me. He said, "If you will do what I ask you to do, I will give you this anointing." He let me see in the Spirit hurting people, hurting churches, the hurting Body of Christ. "I am ready to send great revival," the Lord told me, "and you will need this special anointing because it will draw lost people to you, so that you can witness to them for My sake."

In the Spirit, I saw our own church and many other churches, and I saw cars lined up in all directions trying to get to them. Cars were coming from four

directions – north, south, east and west. I saw people
getting out of their cars and pressing forward trying to get inside the church buildings. I watched as
many were saved, healed, delivered and baptized
in the Spirit.

The Lord said to me, "If you are willing to put
aside everything on your agenda and do what I tell
you, you will reach many for Christ before My return." I was thrilled that He had given me the
opportunity, and I promised Him that I would do
whatever was necessary to see it happen.

After a while, I came to myself, and when I did, I
noticed that oil was beginning to appear on my
hands. I got up, went over to where Ruth was and
showed her. She called it to the attention of the others, and many came by to have a closer look, to see
what exactly was happening to their pastor, and to
try to wipe some of if off on their hands as well.

Next, gold dust began to appear on me. Ruth saw
it on my neck and on my face. I saw it beginning to
fall from the air and land around the altar. I was so
overwhelmed by this manifestation that I could do
nothing but weep. I had just finished telling God
that I was willing to carry this new anointing, and
He was already doing it. He had shown me in the
Spirit that He would give it to me, and here it was
for everyone to see.

The same thing happened on Wednesday morning and, again, on Wednesday night. That night Ruth prophesied over me the exact same thing the Lord had told me that first night.

Just that suddenly, God had added a new element to our ministry. We had experienced the revival fires, but now He was giving us the glory. *Revival Fire and Glory* had met, and we had been launched into a new spiritual level. We were to learn over the coming weeks and months that we had tapped into a whole new wave of revival, a whole new wave of glory that was to sweep across America and the world.

Ruth brought some of her books with her to the meeting, and we began to devour them. What great books! They introduced us further to the glory of God, and I began taking some of them with me wherever I could. People needed to know God's will for this time.

The first book Ruth wrote, *Glory*, has changed lives across the world and, in the process, has become a bestseller. It has been translated into many other languages and its techniques are being used by worship leaders everywhere to lift God's people onto a new level of spiritual encounter. The simple principles she espouses there have revolutionized how we look at worship. For those who have not read the book, they are: Praise ... until the spirit of worship comes. Worship ... until the glory comes. Then ... stand in the glory.

The second book Ruth wrote, *Revival Glory*, describes what happens in revival, documents revival in our time and encourages people everywhere to get into revival. What a blessing it has been!

Early this year *River Glory* was published. This latest book describes the work of the great river of God's Spirit and encourages each of us to jump in and flow with what God is doing today. Sister Ruth was kind enough to include part of my testimony in that book.

I am anxiously awaiting the publication of her next book, *Harvest Glory*. It will contain her stories of spiritual harvest from among the nations during her many years of missionary journeyings. Surely we will all be changed by reading it.

We all fell in love with Ruth and her sweet ministry, and we hated to see her leave us on that Thursday. We were sure, however, that we had tapped into something new and that God was ready to manifest Himself in us and through us.

Chapter

Sixteen

"Just As I Have Been With Moses"

Just as I have been with Moses, I will be with you; I will not fail you or forsake you.

Joshua 1:5

WHEN RUTH LEFT US, SOME WONDERED IF THE MANIFESTATION of God's glory would leave with her. I was convinced that it would not because God had promised it to me personally and had told me He would give it to me if I invited her to my church. If the glory of God was being manifested in Ruth's meetings, why should it not happen in our own as well — even when she was not there?

God honored our faith. Rather than diminish, the manifestation of God's glory continued to expand.

It was that next Sunday morning, when I stood to minister, that my hands were covered with oil, and my clothes were covered with gold dust. That was the day Patsy Burton picked up the gold dust that resulted in the lady at the hospital being healed of cancer and the day Mary Miller combed gold dust from her hair.

Ruth's departure was not to be an ending for us. It was the beginning of greater things to come. God was with us, and He was demonstrating His presence in a new and unusual way.

Chapter

Seventeen

"I Will Pour Forth of My Spirit"

"And it shall come to be in the last days," God says, "that I will pour forth of my Spirit on all mankind."   Acts 2:17

IN JANUARY OF THIS YEAR, I WAS INVITED BY PASTOR BILL Ligon to preach at a meeting in his church, Christian Renewal Church in Brunswick, Georgia. It was a gathering of pastors, evangelists and other staff members. Those people were so hungry. They wanted everything God had for them.

When I began to preach in Christian Renewal Church, the glory of God fell, gold dust began to appear on the carpet and on some of the people. As I laid my hands on the people and they went down in the Spirit, oil began to come from my hands. The people were deeply touched, some were healed, and everyone felt the glory of God.

As a result of that meeting, Pastor Ligon asked me if I could preach a week of revival meetings for him. I agreed, and we started on Valentine's Day, February 14. We did not stop, however, after one week. God was doing such extraordinary things that we went on for another week (Monday through Friday nights) and then another week and another. In each service, God manifested His glory among us with signs, wonders and miracles. His power was so great in those meetings that one night a lady ran into the church to say that a cloud of glory was visible covering the church from the outside.

Unusual healings took place in every service. A chef came forward to be anointed. He had a serious back condition that restricted his movements and kept him in constant pain. God touched his back, and the next day he was out raking leaves from his yard, planting his garden and doing other things that he had not been able to do for a long time.

A lady came forward complaining of terrible pains in her legs. She was unable to function without the use of strong painkillers. She took a prayer cloth from the altar and put it in her stocking. Instantly her leg was healed, and she has had no reoccurrence of the problem since.

Another lady took a prayer cloth for her grandmother who was living in a nursing home. The grandmother had been diagnosed with leukemia. That grandmother was healed.

A pastor from Savannah, Georgia came to be healed of diabetes. His blood sugar level was more than three hundred. God touched him, and when his blood was again tested, it had fallen to less than ninety. It has stayed at that very-acceptable level ever since.

A man from Nashville, Georgia had a bad heart. He came to the meeting, and God healed him.

A pastor from Jacksonville, Florida came for healing for his heart, and he too was healed.

Other amazing things happened. Angels were seen walking throughout the sanctuary during the revival.

The impact all of this had on the people who attended is difficult to describe. Suffice it to say that they were unusually excited and enthusiastically pressed into the services. Some of the men brought *shofars* and blew them during the worship. It was glorious and many lives were changed as a result of the revival, which made a deep impact upon the entire community. We were preaching God's Word and pressing into His anointing, and we expected Him to back us up. We were not disappointed. By April, the meetings were still going strong.

In early April a man brought his little granddaughter to the meetings in Brunswick. She had a compound fracture of her arm. The bone had not penetrated the skin, but it was very close. The arm was so swollen that the attending doctor could not put a cast on it. He put a splint on it and soft wrapped it. Then he told the grandfather, "When the swelling goes down, bring her back, and we'll put a cast on that arm. We may even have to operate, but we can't say for sure at this point."

This grandfather had heard about the miracles God was doing in Brunswick, and he began to believe God for a miracle for his granddaughter.

When he brought her forward in the meeting, he didn't say, "Would you pray for her?" He said, "I brought her to be healed. Preacher, do you believe God will heal her?"

"If I didn't," I told him, "I wouldn't even pray for her. I believe God will heal her right now."

I prayed for the child, and nothing spectacular happened. The next week the man came back and said, "I've got to give a testimony. After you prayed, I took my granddaughter home. The next morning, the swelling was gone, so we took her back to the doctor to get the cast put on. After they had x-rayed the arm, they came back and said, 'She doesn't need the cast. We can't even tell where the arm was broken.' That's what the glory was doing among us.

A six-year-old girl had never spoken a word in her life. Her parents brought her to the meeting. I laid my hands on her, cast out the spirit that bound her, and she began to speak. That girl is still speaking today.

The impact of the miracles done in Brunswick was also felt among pastors, and the number of pastors attending the meetings kept increasing. One night we had more than a hundred pastors in a single service. Some of them had driven from as far away as Florida. When I asked for all the pastors who would like to have this anointing to come forward, more than a hundred of them responded. That's how we knew that more than a hundred were there that night.

Many other churches were impacted by the Brunswick Revival, not only as a result of these pastors attending and being blessed, but by lay people being blessed and taking this blessing out to other places.

Many hundreds of people have been saved in these meetings. Someone was recently telling me the details of the conversion of an alcoholic who came into one of those meetings. He was very restless during the service and was talking a lot, but when I began preaching he got very quiet and listened carefully to everything I had to say. When I had finished my message and given the altar call, the man ran to the altar. I gave him a word of knowledge that he needed deliverance, and he needed salvation. He accepted God's diagnosis of his problem. After I cast a devil of alcoholism out of him, he gave his heart to Christ and became a totally new creature.

It was the manifestation of God's glory in the form of the gold dust and the supernatural oil that caused it all to happen, and many took this blessing home with them.

When a school teacher came a very long distance to attend, I was led to tell her that she was going to receive this anointing. At first, she didn't believe it. Her father was unsaved, and he had been telling her that this manifestation was fake. He got a big laugh out of the whole matter.

The next day as she was applying her makeup she noticed that she had gold dust on her face. It began to appear in her house and in her school on her desk. She called other teachers to see it, and they got very excited. Her father now believes — since it happened to his daughter.

After seven continuous weeks of revival in Brunswick, we were still going strong and were experiencing some awesome services.

Chapter

Eighteen

"You Will Spread Abroad"

Enlarge the place of your tent; Stretch out the curtains of your dwellings, spare not; Lengthen your cords And strengthen your pegs. For you will spread abroad to the right and to the left. And your descendants will possess nations And will resettle the desolate cities. Isaiah 54:2-3

BEFORE I TOOK ON THE BRUNSWICK REVIVAL, I HAD accepted a series of meetings in Indiana, Michigan and Canada, so I took a few days off from the revival and fulfilled this commitment. God manifested His glory in each place.

First I spoke for a few days at New Creations, a ministry in Richmond, Indiana headed by Tim and

Bonnie Cummings. They have a boarding school for wayward kids. Those young people have been involved in everything: drugs, theft to support a drug habit, dealing drugs to support a drug habit, prostitution to support a drug habit, auto theft, grand larceny, robbery, burglary, etc. While I was there, the gold dust fell, and dozens of those teenagers came forward to receive Jesus Christ as their Savior.

From Richmond, Indiana, I went to Three Rivers, Michigan, to Faith Christian Fellowship. Pastors came there from many other states: Ohio, Tennessee, Kentucky, Indiana, Illinois, Michigan and Iowa, as well as from Canada. As I was preaching, the gold dust fell, and the oil began to flow. These men and women were hungry for God's anointing, and they pressed in to receive it. Many of those pastors received the anointing of gold dust and oil in their own lives.

From there I went to Walpole Island, to a Chippewa Indian reservation, and preached for Pastor Larry Gilbert, whose brother is the Chief of the Chippewa. Many of the Chippewas were saved and healed. The glory of God came down, and the gold dust came upon me.

From there, I went to Lemington, Ontario, Canada (on Lake Erie), to the Lemington Christian Center and ministered with Pastor Dan Tamburo and his family. Gold dust and oil was manifested in our services with the Tamburos, and everyone present in the service ended up on the floor, slain under the power of God.

At one point I noticed that music continued to flow from the keyboard, although I thought everyone was on their faces before God. I looked up to see where Katy Tamburo, the pastor's daughter, was. She was normally the one playing the keyboard. I thought I had seen her on the floor too. There she was, still on her face before the Lord. I turned to the pastor and asked him who was playing the keyboard. He looked and said in return, "I don't see anyone." Still, the keyboard continued to play. God was supernaturally providing our worship music.

Before long angels began to sing as well. We could hear their voices although we could not see them. It was so glorious that people were running in off of the streets to get saved. Because of these manifestations, many sinners came to Christ. People were rushing to get down the aisles to the altar to pray.

One man who was an alcoholic ran out of the service because he couldn't stand the awesome convicting power of the Spirit of God. When he got home, he tried to drink some more but could not get drunk. He got back in his car, drove to the church, ran down the aisle and got saved.

A young lady, also on drugs, did exactly the same thing. She was afraid of what she was seeing and what she was feeling and turned and left. When she got home, she smoked some crack, but she, too, found that she could not get high, and she returned to the church and got saved.

During the days I was there, supernatural oil and gold dust were not only seen throughout the church. It was all over the pastor's desk. After I left the pastor found gold dust on his fireplace at home and also on the chimney. God is doing unusual things to show us His mighty power.

Now Pastor Dan is flowing in this ministry, and his church is full. He is one of the finest men I have ever met in my life, and he has a wonderful family as well.

Recently, Pastor Dan called me to say that it was still happening. He is excited and is pressing into this new move of God, this new anointing of the Holy Spirit, and is having more people saved in the church than ever before.

While I was in Lemington, and Pastor Dan introduced me to a barbecue place there that had the best ribs I have ever eaten. As we witnessed to some of the people in the restaurant that day, our waitress came to Christ. This, to me, is the whole reason behind God's sending these unusual manifestations into our midst.

Chapter

Nineteen

"Those Who Hunger and Thirst"

Blessed are those who hunger and thirst for righteousness, for they shall be satisfied.

Matthew 5:6

SOME OF THE OTHER BAPTIST PASTORS WHO HAD ALREADY received the baptism of the Holy Spirit became interested in the new manifestations of the gold dust and the supernatural oil and asked me to come to their churches. The only problem was that there didn't seem to be time. I was traveling back to Austell every weekend to be in my church, so there were no nights free. In the end, we made a decision to reduce the number of nights of the meeting in Brunswick to Wednesday through Friday, and that would give me two nights for other places. Miraculously, this didn't seem to hurt our crowds in Brunswick. In fact, it seemed to help them.

Pastor Eddie Rogers, as before, was one of the first to want this new blessing. His church, by now, was known as Sweet Spirit Fellowship and had moved from Hiram to Dallas, Georgia.

Eddie had just finished some meetings with a very well known evangelist, but the first night of our meetings with him Eddie said the crowd was the biggest ever. This demonstrated how hungry people are to see the glory of God.

Before the service that Monday night, while the two of us were praying in Eddie's office, gold dust began to appear, not only on me, but also on him, on his desk and on the floor. We could feel the power of God falling on us. Then oil began to flow. I knew that we were going to have a great service that night.

Eddie did a wonderful job leading us all in worship, and during the worship service we could see the golden rain coming down. It was falling on the seats of the church, on the carpets and on the people. When it came time for the altar call, the people pressed forward to receive from God.

I prayed for everyone who was there that night, and many of them had gold dust appearing on them. Quite a few of them told me that gold dust has been appearing on them ever since.

It was at Eddie's that we started having something new, gold and silver fillings in people's teeth. We had heard of this happening at other times and places, but we had never experienced it ourselves until then. That night fillings were appearing in gold and in silver, and the dust was raining down on us in gold, in silver and in something that appeared to be ruby red.

These manifestations are all highly unusual and it is not surprising that they spark heated controversy. One of the great women prophets of America explained the gold fillings in this way: She said God is just taking back what the devil stole. When Adolph Hitler was killing the Jewish people all across Europe, he pulled their gold teeth and stole their precious jewelry. When God gives us back precious things, He is saying, "I am taking back what the devil has stolen and returning it to my people." He wants everyone to know that we are His people, so He is manifesting His glory among us. What an awesome day in which we live!

After it happened at Eddie's, we began to experience it in Brunswick too. A man called me not long ago from the upper part of Georgia and told me the following story. He and his pastor had been in a small revival meeting in an Episcopalian church in Smyrna, Georgia, and a couple got up and testified that they had been in one of my meetings. Both of them had cancer. I laid hands on them, and not only were they healed of the cancer, but they discovered gold fillings in their teeth, gold dust appeared on them, and oil came from their hands.

When the couple gave this testimony in Smyrna, gold dust appeared on the evangelist who was there preaching in that small Episcopalian church that was so hungry for the touch of God, and it appeared on the couple who were giving the testimony as well. The aspect of the gold fillings, which seems to be happening more and more around the country, began for me that first night of revival meeting I preached at Eddie's church.

Several people were divinely healed in that service: people in pain, people in stress, people in great need.

On Tuesday night, the process was repeated all over again.

What made me as happy as anything else about the outpouring of God's glory at Sweet Spirit Fellowship was that Eddie got it himself and could carry it on. I have never ceased to be amazed at the power that is transmitted through the laying on of hands.

Since that time, Eddie has gone out to several other places to preach, and in each place these same manifestations have accompanied him. He has had dynamic meetings in which gold dust has fallen and teeth have been miraculously filled.

Eddie calls me several times a week, and we rejoice to share experiences of what God is doing in our respective ministries.

Keith Ellis was another of those who was blessed by this phenomenon. He lost more than half of his congregation after he was baptized in the Holy Ghost at Eddie's church, and even some of those who stayed with him were still rather skeptical. Since I was the one responsible for getting him involved in this, he asked me to come and minister to his people.

I went to Keith's church, and we had an awesome meeting. We had some wonderful healings there. Keith has had beginnings of gold dust appear on him, and God is using him.

I was invited to another Baptist church near Brunswick, and God did so many miracles there that two doctors and one doctor's wife were all saved in a single service. People of many denominations were saved in that church.

One lady came running down the aisle saying, "I have been in a Baptist church all my life, and I just realized that I am not saved." God's anointing of glory makes people everywhere do that.

Not everyone was happy with what God was doing. One lady left the church quite insulted. "This is a Baptist church," she said, "and this is not a Baptist meeting." She vowed that she would never go back.

In May the pastor called me to say that he had heard from the lady. She had been troubled by the Spirit since the day she had walked out of the church and could find no rest. She asked his forgiveness, vowed to no longer resist what God was doing, and came back to the church.

Chapter

Twenty

"So That You Might Believe"

*Therefore many other signs Jesus also performed in the presence of the disciples, which are not written in this book; but these have been written so that you may believe that Jesus is the Christ, the Son of God; and that believing you may have life in His name.*John 20:30-31

TO ME, THE GREATEST THING ABOUT THE MANIFESTATION of the glory of God in my life has been the fact that it draws men and women to Christ. What Jesus did on Earth, He did so that we would believe, and I am convinced that the purpose of God's glory being manifested is so that more people will come to the feet of Jesus.

Jesus declared that signs, wonders and miracles would follow the preaching of the Gospel, but those signs, wonders and miracles were for a definite purpose. That purpose was to draw men and women to Christ.

As God manifested His power in my life in this new way, I began seeing thousands of people getting saved, coming to know the Lord Jesus Christ as their Savior.

When the Lord spoke to me that first night when Ruth Heflin ministered to us and told me that He would give me this anointing, He made it clear that the purpose was to draw the lost to Him, and it has done just that. He showed me those lines of people trying to get into churches, and the wonderful thing about the visible glory of God is that it does indeed draw men and women.

I had always been a soul-winner. Our church had consistently appeared in the top three percent of churches in the entire Southern Baptist Convention for reaching people for Jesus. Every year we had gotten letters of commendation for our work of soul-winning. Still we wanted to do more.

We were already baptizing two hundred or more new believers every year, but we were not satisfied. When six thousand, five hundred people had come back to the Lord in our twenty-four-week revival meeting, we were happy for that, and we called churches in the areas where they lived and referred them to a local church they could attend. That was wonderful, but we were not satisfied and wanted to do more.

We had been recognized by the president of our conventions, both national and state, as being leaders in evangelism and had been written about in the much-acclaimed book *Effective Evangelistic Churches* by Thom Rainer, but we were still not satisfied. We were sure there were thousands of lost people in our community, and we knew there were millions more around the world who needed Christ. We wanted to do more.

Now, as the manifestation of the gold dust, the supernatural oil and the gold fillings progressed, we were winning more people than we ever had before. Men and women, boys and girls were being drawn to Christ in large numbers.

What thrilled me even more than this, however, was to see people being saved in public places — out where the sinners are. We have always known that we must reach people beyond the church doors, and the visible manifestation of God's glory has opened up a means of doing that very effectively.

I went into a large department store, for instance, and a girl was working the cash register. She had quite a line waiting on her, and she grew very irritable. "You know," I began when it came my turn,

"Jesus loves you." She looked at me and started crying.

"What's the matter?" I asked.

"Just this morning," she said, "I was so down, so depressed, that I told God that if He really loved me, and I really had a future, to send someone to the store today to tell me. You just said it."

I led that girl in a sinner's prayer, and she accepted Jesus right there in the store. People around us began to applaud when they saw what was happening.

When I went into a mall one day in Brunswick, a lady said to me, "Can I help you?"

"Yes," I said, "I'm looking for the lost."

"Do you mean the Lost and Found?" she asked.

"No Ma'am," I answered. "Those who are found are okay. I'm looking for those who are lost."

"What do you mean?" she asked.

I asked her, "Do you know Jesus?" and she, too, began to weep.

I led her to the Lord, and she was saved right there.

"That's what I'm talking about," I told her, "that's what I'm looking for."

I spoke to a waitress who was serving at the Golden Corral Restaurant in Brunswick, asking her if she knew Jesus. She didn't, and I was able to lead her to the Lord.

God has saved so many people in restaurants recently that I have gotten in the habit of doing something a little strange. It started one day when I was in a restaurant in Florida with another pastor. He said to me, "These people look like they need the Lord. I wish we could get them into church."

Just then the Lord said to me, "Preach to them here."

I said to the other pastor, "I feel like the Lord wants us to preach to them right here."

"That's fine," he said, "but how are we going to get their attention?"

I suddenly had an idea. I got up on a chair and said in a loud voice, "I'm in love with a Man ..."

People stopped eating and turned my way. Waitresses stopped in their tracks. The manager came out to see what was happening. As he was coming toward me, I said, "And I'm going to marry Him ..."

It just happened that this manager had been in our meetings and had heard me talk about a new boldness I was experiencing in God that had enabled me to witness in public places. He came over closer to me and said, "You're fixing to do it, aren't you?"

"If you don't mind, I am," I answered.

"Well, go to it," he said.

So, I continued, "And that man's name is Jesus."

I preached ten or fifteen minutes about Him. One after another, the people in the restaurant came to me to be led to Christ as their Savior. The pastor who was with me stood there and wept and the manager stood and wept with him. It was a powerful scene.

I have never read where they did that in the Bible, and it may sound really stupid to some, but it felt awfully good winning those people to Christ, and I don't regret having done it in the least.

One day while I was praying in the motel in Brunswick, preparing for the service, oil and gold dust got all over the floor of the motel room where I was praying and praising God. When the maid came, she said, "Oh my, what's all this?"

I said, "That's the glory of God."

"It is?" she asked, obviously startled.

"Do you know the Lord?" I asked.

"Well, I know about Him," she said.

"Are you saved?" I insisted.

"Well, I know about Him," she repeated.

I tried a different tactic: "If you died right now, would you go to Heaven?"

"I know about the Lord," she repeated for the third time.

"Then where is Jesus?" I asked.

She answered, "He's in Heaven."

"You're not saved," I assured her and proceeded to lead her to Christ.

When we had finished praying, I asked, "Now, where's Jesus?"

"He's in my heart," she responded, and you could tell that it was true.

"Now you're saved!" I affirmed.

Soon the lady went about her business, but before long there was a knock at the door and someone said, "Housekeeping."

"They've already cleaned this room," I said through the door.

"It's me," she said, "and I need to talk to you."

I opened the door, and she had her sister with her. The sister worked there too.

"My sister's not saved either," she said, and I led her sister to Christ, and they left.

About the time I was ready to leave for the service, another knock came at the door. "Who is it?" I called.

"It's housekeeping," was the answer.

When I opened the door there were four teenagers and two grown men standing with the two women. These were their children and their husbands. None of them were saved, and I led them all to the Lord.

I don't mind being looked at as strange if I can do something for the lost of this world. That might bother some people, but not me. In the past six months, I have been able to lead more than two thousand people to the feet of Jesus. Many of those have been baptized in the Holy Ghost and many have received an anointing for themselves, and gold dust has come upon them.

Why is the gold dust so helpful in winning the lost? It compels men and women to listen. It compels them to make a decision concerning the kingdom. It is time for us to get out of the flesh and let God do the witnessing to people around us.

God is saving many people who have been hardened. They are coming to the Lord now because of the signs, wonders and miracles He is doing among us. He is saving people who have been under heavy oppression. Over the past months, many people have come to me and reported that depression has left them. The manifestation of the glory of God has given them hope, when they thought all hope was lost. This experience is life-changing.

The manifestation of God's glory is helping many others win the lost as well. A pastor called me from New Jersey. He had tried my I-love-a-man trick and, because of it, had been able to witness to some people in a restaurant. While he was witnessing to them, gold dust came on both him and them, and supernatural oil flowed from his hands. He was able to win them to the Lord Jesus Christ. I have received calls just like that from many parts of the United States.

One lady called me in late April from a motel in Brunswick. She was staying there while attending the revival. When her maid came in, she discovered that she had some serious problems, and she was able to minister to her. She led her to the Lord and prayed with her about her problems. Gold dust appeared and oil ran from her hands.

Even when I'm off preaching in revivals, the Lord has convicted my heart that I need to be out witnessing to people, and I do. I go from business to business and house to house. I've been doing that in Brunswick for many weeks.

When I go out, I ask God to make me sensitive to the needs of those around me. When I sit down to eat in any restaurant, God either shows me that the waitress is spiritually okay, or He tells me to witness to her. We have been winning airline stewardesses, and men and women from law enforcement, fire and rescue services, public safety and the military. Because of the many miracles God is doing in our ministry, I have been able to witness to many people in the medical profession. Doctors, nurses, technicians and lab workers listen when their patients are healed. My personal goal is to win ten people every day to Jesus, and I would prefer to win many more than that.

I volunteer my time to serve as chaplain with several different law enforcement agencies in our area, and I am called when any officer is injured or killed or traumatized. This gives me an opportunity to witness to many people. I have also had the privilege of speaking in several high schools, where I find teenagers are ready for a radical revival.

All of us can be soul winners.

In mid-May, when I was doing a revival in Darrien, Georgia, at Coastal Christian Center, a family brought in a young man. He had been hitch-hiking, and the Lord told them to pick him up. They took him home, let him take a shower in their house, fed him, and then brought him to church. That night he got saved.

I encourage people to be very cautious about pick-ing up hitchhikers, but when the Lord tells you to pull over and talk to someone, you need to do it. These are wonderful times we are living in, for people are very hungry for the Lord. The signs and wonders of God's Spirit work as a catalyst to draw hungry hearts to God. Let us win them anywhere and everywhere we can.

Recently, we shared a story in our church bulle-tin, and I would like to share it with you too:

One day a woman named Louise fell asleep in her bed and dreamed a very fitful dream. She dreamed that someone in Hell wrote a letter to her, and it was to be delivered to her by a mes-senger. The messenger passed between the lakes of burning fire and brimstone that occupy Hell and found his way to the door that would lead him to the outside world.

Louise dreamed that the messenger walked to her house, came inside and gently, but firmly woke her up. He gave her the message, saying only that a friend had written it to her from Hell.

Louise, in her dream, with trembling hands, took the letter and read:

My Friend,

I stand in Judgment now,
And feel that you're to blame somehow,
On earth, I walked with you day by day,
And never did you point the way.

You knew the Lord in truth and glory,
But never did you tell the story.
My knowledge then was very dim;
You could have led me safe to Him.

Though we lived together on the Earth,
You never told me of the second birth,
And now I stand this day condemned,
Because you failed to mention Him.

You taught me many things, that's true,
I called you "friend" and trusted you,
But I learn now that it's too late,
You could have kept me from this fate.

We walked by day and talked by night,
And yet you showed me not the Light.
You let me live, and love and die.
You knew I'd never live on high.

Yes, I called you a 'friend' in life.
And trusted you through joy and strife.
And yet on coming to the end,
I cannot, now, call you "My Friend."

The letter was signed "Marsha"

After reading the letter, Louise awoke. The dream was still real in her mind, and sweat dripped from her body in pools. She swore she could still smell the acrid brimstone from her room. As she contemplated the meaning of her dream, she realized that as a Christian, she had failed in her duty to *"go out to all the world and preach the Gospel."* As she thought of that, she promised herself that the next day she would call Marsha and invite her to go to church with her.

The next morning she called Marsha and this was the conversation:

"Bill, is Marsha there?"

"Louise, you don't know?"

"No, Bill, know what?"

"Marsha was killed last night in a car accident. I thought you knew."

— Author unknown

The Scriptures warn us:

When I say to the wicked, "You will surely die,"
and you do not warn him or speak out to warn

the wicked from his wicked way that he may
live, that wicked man shall die in his iniquity,
but his blood I will require at your hand.

Ezekiel 3:18

Surely we will not stand guiltless before God if we have kept silent in this life about the most important issue, life and death, eternity with Christ or without Him. Let the glory of God make you a great soul-winner today.

Chapter

Twenty-One

"The Laying On of Hands"

*Do not neglect the spiritual gift within you,
which was bestowed on you through prophetic
utterance with the laying on of hands by the
presbytery.* 1 Timothy 4:14

WHEN RUTH HEFLIN INVITED ME TO SPEAK AT THE
Men's Convention in Ashland, Virginia, I welcomed
the opportunity. I wanted to be around her, around
her anointed mother, Rev. Edith Ward Heflin,
around her anointed Uncle, Dr. William A. Ward,
and around the anointed staff of their campground.
I knew we were going to have a wonderful meeting, but just how wonderful I could not have
imagined.

In the first service, on Friday morning, Brother Mike Greer spoke, and the power of God fell in that place. I was determined that I was going to have his hands laid on me, but when the altar call was given, the rest of the men ran so quickly to the front that I could find no place to squeeze in among them. I kept saying to the Lord, "Lord, let him look over my way." When he finally did look my way, and I got him to lay hands on me, I felt more power from God than I had ever felt before.

Many people sit back on the periphery of spiritual activity and, by refusing to get into what God is doing at the moment, they miss out on it. Then, because they didn't get it, all they know to do is criticize. This is sad. I want all that God has for me, and I am determined to press into His glory and receive more and more.

When it came my time to speak that night, I felt very humbled. I was in the presence of men (and women) of great spiritual stature, but God helped me. A man came to me that next morning and said, "I was ready to quit the ministry and had even thought of ending my life, but the manifestation of the oil and the gold dust I saw here last night and this morning and the words you have spoken have greatly encouraged me. I now know that God is real, and I intend to take it all home with me and live it in my own life."

At the close of that morning service, when Brother Ward laid hands on me, I felt something like a bolt of lightning coming over me. Thousands of volts of Holy Ghost electricity hit me. I knew in that moment that I could resist what I was feeling and not receive anything, or I could press in and have a whole new anointing. I had no desire to resist. It was wonderful, and I came away from that convention with a new touch of God upon my life.

Being with Ruth Heflin those couple of days made me realize what a great team we would make, and we quickly made plans to do some conferences and some television interviews together.

Many ministers seem to be too proud to confess that they need more of God, but I know that this anointing is catching. It is imparted by one person to another, and we can all have a portion of it.

I personally received great blessing through the laying on of the hands of men like Billy Graham, Ciff Barrows, Adrian Rogers, Dan Duke, Norman Robertson, Paul Walker, Jamie Buckingham, Michael Thompson, Charles and Frances Hunter, Rodney Howard-Browne, Jessie Duplantis, Jerry Savelle, Carey Robertson, John Kilpatrick, Steve Hill, Bill Ligon and now Ruth Heflin and William A. Ward.

There is something good that comes to us through the laying on of hands. I am determined to have all I can get, and I encourage you to do the same.

Chapter

Twenty-Two

"I Will Do Something New"

Behold, I will do something new,
Now it will spring forth;   Isaiah 43:19

WITH ALL OF MY TRAVELS AND MINISTRY ELSEWHERE, GOD has continued to move at Friendship Baptist Church. We recently had a lady come forward for prayer at the altar call who was covered with cancer. I laid my hands on her, and she went down so hard in the Spirit that the first three rows behind her went down too. When she got up, she said, "I felt my healing come." Tests were later run, and her doctor confirmed that she was completely healed. That lady, Helen Mann, is eighty-two years old, is a missionary to Mexico, and has built more than a hundred churches in that country.

A man who came forward had suffered a massive heart attack. Sixty percent of his heart had been damaged. He had five heart blockages and was scheduled to have surgery. I laid my hands on him in the name of Jesus and felt the power of God fall. When the man went into the hospital for surgery, doctors ran dye through his arteries and heart to check the blockages. They informed him that the blockages were no longer there and that his heart was restored as though he had never had a heart attack.

Greater things were yet to be seen. On Sunday evening, May 2, some people brought a six-year-old crippled girl to the service. This child had never walked. When I asked them how the child's legs had been mangled, they told me that she had been born that way.

Before I ever prayed for her, I knew that she was going to walk. Gold dust was falling like rain in the church, and I could see it on her. Oil was dripping from my hands, and I knew that God was going to do the miracle for us.

I told the girl, "You're going to walk."

I laid my hands on her and prayed, and then I said to her, "Now walk! Walk!"

Two or three people got her by the hands and started trying to help her take some steps.

Myrna Thompson, one of my praise team members, later told me, "I was watching, and I saw those little legs straightening out."

Within a few minutes, that girl began to walk, and then she began to run.

A lady named Jane had been fighting some unknown disease for two years already. Doctors had run every conceivable test on her and had eventually concluded that it must be a type of cancer. They gave her very little hope of recovery. The cancer had spread throughout her body. When everything else failed, Jane decided to give divine healing a try.

In May, she came to our church and came down to the altar to get anointed. "I came to be healed," she said. I laid hands on her and prayed over her, and the Lord touched her. I could feel the rush of the power of God going into her. She came back the next week to testify that she was totally healed.

She had brought a Jewish lady in a wheelchair with her, and, as a result of Jane's miraculous healing, the Jewish lady accepted Christ as her personal Savior and became a Messianic Jew.

When I had been caught up to Heaven in November of 1998, God had told me that when the supernatural oil was flowing from my hands, I was to lay hands on sick people, and they would be healed. He was keeping His promise.

Several weeks before that one of the brothers in Brunswick who has a gift of prophecy had foretold this event. He prophesied that in the eighth week of the revival, I would lay hands on a cripple and that cripple would walk and then run. The Lord said through him that the healing of the cripple would provide a new spark for the revival, a new beginning, a new dimension for us to flow in. From that point on, the Lord said, we would see many more healings, many more people saved and many more people delivered. We were about to see this anointed prophecy come to pass.

Chapter

Twenty-Three

"I Bore You On Eagles' Wings"

You yourselves have seen what I did to the Egyptians, and how I bore you on eagles' wings, and brought you to Myself.   Exodus 19:4

IN MAY SISTER RUTH HEFLIN ARRANGED FOR ME TO minister with her in a campmeeting outside of Dallas, Texas, with Evangelist Dwight Jones. When we got to Dallas, Ruth was housed in one building of a motel there, and I was in another. As the both of us were praying in our respective rooms, preparing for the service that night, gold dust began to appear — on the carpets and on us — and golden oil began to flow from our hands.

We stopped at a restaurant to eat on our way to

the meeting, and gold dust was falling as we sat there at our table. I used the opportunity to witness to everyone around us. Most of those we spoke with that night were already saved, but they were blessed to see what God was doing. They also said they were happy to meet people who were not ashamed to witness for the Lord in public places.

By the time we got to the place of service, the manifestation of the gold dust and the oil was awesome. While we were sitting on the platform that night, golden dust fell like rain upon the place. The service was glorious.

A lady came forward saying that she had been in horrendous pain for many weeks. A doctor told her that she had spurs on her spine. "Let's let God supernaturally remove the spurs," I told her, "and the pain will leave." I laid hands on her, and she went down in the Spirit.

A little later she came up to the podium and asked if she could testify. "The pain is gone," she said, "so I know the spurs are gone."

People were pressing in to have hands laid on them to receive this anointing. What an awesome God we serve!

A pastor said to me, "You have renewed me. What God did through you has renewed my ministry and has given me new hope."

A medical doctor came up for prayer and asked

me to lay hands on him. When I did, gold dust appeared on him and supernatural oil came into his palms. I said, "Sir, you're going to bless many people. You will now minister supernaturally to those who will receive it. To those who want it in the natural, minister to them in the natural. But God will use you in a mighty way." He and his wife were so glad that God had chosen them that they shouted for joy.

Many other similar great things happened in that service.

I was only able to be in that one service at the campmeeting because we were scheduled to be interviewed for an hour that next day on the Daystar Television Network out of Dallas. Marcus Lamb and his wife Joni interviewed Sister Ruth and me. During the program, there was gold dust all over us, and many people called in because they were challenged by this manifestation.

God gave me a word during the time we were on the air that a certain pastor was watching the program, and that he was very discouraged and ready to abandon his ministry. If that man would take the step of faith of laying his hand on his television set and praying with us, God would deliver him, and he would receive the visible anointing of gold dust and supernatural oil. I asked the man to call in, so that his deliverance could be confirmed.

The four of us agreed together that this man would be restored and encouraged and anointed as never before, so that his ministry would experience a whole new lease on life.

Sure enough, a pastor called in to say that he was the man I was talking about. Everything I had spoken happened to him as we prayed.

Many other people were ministered to through the program, and the telephones did not stop ringing the entire time.

The program was so blessed, in fact, and there was so much response that at the end of the scheduled hour of interview, Marcus decided to extend the time for another hour. We continued on for another hour, and many more calls came in.

I was led to share testimonies about people who had been raised from the dead and those who had been healed of cancer. I assured our listeners that cancer cannot live where the presence of Jesus is. It cannot live where the anointing is. The anointing is better than radiation and chemotherapy.

I had to leave the station and rush to the airport to get my flight back to Georgia for my scheduled revival services in Brunswick. Sister Ruth was going to tape another segment, but I had only thirty minutes to catch my flight.

I was on a non-ticketed flight, and I didn't have a seat, so I needed to get there in time, and I made it.

My flight was scheduled to take off at two fifty in the afternoon and to get me into Atlanta at five fifty-five. I was hoping to get a good night's rest at home before I headed off to Brunswick the next day.

I had heard the news the night before about tornadoes slashing through Oklahoma City, Wichita Falls and at other places in that area. Many people had been killed, and property damage was extremely high. I hadn't thought about this weather phenomenon, which some were already calling "the weather phenomenon of the century," affecting our air travel, but soon after I got to the airport I was told to expect delays. Flights had been suspended during the tornado period, and they were backed up. Some planes, I learned, had sat on the runway for several hours, waiting for clearance to take off.

After I sat there waiting on my flight for several hours, it was announced that the plane we were scheduled to board had been delayed in Houston. The agent at the counter told us that the plane had encountered some sort of mechanical problem, and the flight would have to be cancelled. We might as well look for a hotel room, we were told, and plan on flying the next morning instead.

I knew that I had to be in Brunswick the next day, and as I prayed, God assured me that I would indeed get on a plane that same day and be able to get home, get some rest and get to my meetings on time.

About the time God spoke that to me, I noticed a lady who was talking to an airline representative at the counter. She was from New York, and her mother had passed away, so she was trying to get to New York with her husband and children. She had become very discouraged, and was crying and upset because she had been told that no more planes would be flying that night.

I said to the lady, "Don't worry about it. God has spoken to me that I'm going to Atlanta tonight. You can make your connection to New York from there. Let's pray together and claim it."

We did that, and then I went back to the agent and said, "We'll be right over here when the plane gets in to take us to Atlanta."

He said, "Sir, there is only one more flight coming in from Atlanta tonight, and it will not be going back out until six thirty in the morning. You might as well go to a motel and get some sleep."

"No," I said, "that flight is going to turn around and take us back to Atlanta. We'll be waiting over there."

We stayed right there, believing God for a miracle. About eleven that night it was announced that the flight from Atlanta was arriving and that because of the many delays people had suffered throughout the day it would be returning to Atlanta with those who had valid tickets. The plane was large enough to take people from several other cancelled flights.

We went to the ticket counter and had our tickets changed, and, as God had said, we flew to Atlanta that night. It was a double miracle, for Atlanta had also been experiencing bad weather, and both trains and planes had been suffering delays.

I got home, got a good night's sleep and drove the five hours to Brunswick the following day to begin our eighth week of revival.

The enemy had done everything he could to prevent me from being there, but God had intervened, and I was confident that the coming week of revival would be our greatest.

Chapter

Twenty-Four

"Increasing In Strength"

But Saul kept increasing in strength and confounding the Jews who lived at Damascus by proving that this Jesus is the Christ.

Acts 9:22

AS THE EIGHTH WEEK OF REVIVAL BEGAN IN BRUNSWICK, we knew that God was about to do unusual miracles for us, to take us to a new level of anointing. I was excited as I made my way to Brunswick from my home in Austell. God had brought to pass the first part of the prophecy, and I knew that He would do the rest.

Others, too, seemed to sense the excitement of what God was about to do. People flew in from many places to participate in the revival. Others came long distances by bus and whole vanloads of people appeared, wanting to be blessed. That week we had the largest crowds ever.

We had increased not only in numbers. The people were praising and worshiping God as never before. Many were walking or running around the inside of the building, and, as they did, many were receiving miracles of healing.

That night we told people to put their hands on their mouths and to believe God for the healing of bad teeth. I did not ask God for gold fillings. I prayed that He would heal abscesses, take out cavities and resolve any other dental problems people had.

Several people came up to me later and said that God had healed their teeth. When they opened their mouths to show me, I found that they had received gold fillings. Some had gold bridges or gold caps.

There were many people in that service who had arthritis. I could see the knots in their hands as I prayed for them. I was believing God for the knots to go, and after prayer it happened. Their fingers flew open, all the knots disappeared, and the people were totally healed.

I always encourage people to consult with their doctors, and in many cases they come back to say that their doctors have taken them off their medications. When God heals us, the miracle will stand the test of examination.

Seventy-five percent of the people in the Brunswick meeting that Friday night had gold dust on them, and oil was coming from their hands.

One of the greatest miracles God did that week was of the restoration of a native American minister by the name of Robert Freeman. He had begun preaching very early in life, and God had used him in great miracles. After he was married and had several children, however, he had a terrible automobile accident one night on the way home from a preaching engagement. His wife was instantly killed, and his own body was left badly broken.

He was in traction in the Intensive Care Unit for forty days and when he finally left the hospital, doctors did not expect him to survive. Over the coming months and years, he was in and out of twelve different hospitals in twelve different cities, tended by thirty-five different doctors. In all, he made six hundred and fifty trips to the hospital.

Eventually, it was decided that his accident and the resulting trauma had caused a chemical imbalance in his body and brought on a severe case of bipolar disease. He was now diagnosed as manic depressive and placed on prescription drugs.

His life from that point on was a continual struggle. In his debilitated condition, he was expected to serve as both father and mother to his children. He knew that he had a call to the ministry, and he did recover enough to conduct some revival meetings around the south, but somehow he had lost his vision and felt totally burned out.

He remarried, and his wife Cheryl was a solid influence on his life. When she heard about the revival in Brunswick, she encouraged him to attend.

"Gold dust?" he said. "I'm not going to those meetings. I have seen God heal the sick, raise the dead, open blinded eyes and cause the deaf to hear, but gold dust ...? No way!"

They were invited to a birthday party in Brunswick, and the people at that party were talking about the revival and about what God was doing at Christian Renewal Church. On their way home that night, Cheryl pleaded with him to go to the revival meeting. She said that she was believing God to heal him and was planning to leave her job so that they could travel more for the Lord.

He was thinking just the opposite. He had already sold his Gospel tent and he was in the process of selling his amplifying system. He wanted out. He was tired.

He finally consented to go to the meeting, but he insisted that they sit on the very back row of the church. They were sitting back there minding their own business when I was led to send someone to ask them to come sit up front. They did.

While Cheryl stood and worshiped, he sat and

sulked, but before long he began to feel something. He said it was "a lot of love."

I was led to write on one of my cards and to send a message down to him. It said: "The work of God that is shut up in your heart will become a burning fire for God as you begin to speak it out. I heard from the Lord that you are weary of holding it in. Many lost people are waiting for the Word to burst forth from you. They will run to the altar to surrender. Go forth without fear."

He handed the card to Cheryl, and she read it and began to cry. "That's for us," she said. "That's for us. That's for us."

He listened carefully to what I had to say that night, and when I called for those who needed prayer, he responded.

Although many went to the altar for prayer, I went to him first. "Sir," I began, "someone has hurt you badly, but God is healing the hurt in your life. I see you standing and preaching the Gospel of Jesus Christ. You are going to speak the Word, and whatever you have need of, God is going to give it to you at that moment. You won't have to struggle, you won't have to fight as you begin to preach."

He was still very skeptical of the oil and the gold dust, but he could see them flowing, and he began to sense that it was indeed the glory of God. There was a great anointing upon me that night.

He later told me that God said to him, "I'm walking in this man, and he's walking in Me. I'm working through him, and whatever you have need of, son, I'll give it to you."

The couple left the service that night thinking that it had been good to be there, that they were still not sure of what they had seen but that they definitely wanted to go back. The fact that he agreed to go back surprised Cheryl, but she was thrilled about it.

The next night I spoke to him again, this time about a great hunger, about a great ministry, about preaching to the Indian nations (he was part Cherokee, as I am.) There seemed to be a kindred spirit between us, as if we had known each other for years, and he responded as I ministered to him. God said to him, "I will anoint you and use you. I will not turn you aside or turn you away. Only love me." As I prayed for him, the oil and the gold came upon me.

They came back a third time. He later described what happened: "God began to minister to me, and I found myself suddenly walking in this anointing and feeling the miracle flow of the river of God's glory in life. Then I began to see the oil and the gold. That's when I knew for sure that it was from God. Satan would never do that.

"God sent pastor Bob Shattles into my life for a reason. God used him to pray for me, to minister to me. My vision was gone, but now revival fires have been sparked in my soul and it has birthed a new anointing in me. Now this same anointing is flowing in my own life, and I see souls coming to Christ.

"It's terrible to feel burned out. It's terrible to feel that there is no place for you in the ministry anymore. I thank God for this man because his anointing has brought restoration to me personally and to my ministry.

"I was in the process of selling all my evangelistic equipment, but now I am again carrying this Gospel — into the streets, into football stadiums, into civic centers and in city-wide crusades.

"I pray for Pastor Shattles every day that God will bless him and give him thousands of souls for his hire, and I pray for the revival in Brunswick and for Pastor Bill Ligon, who has shown me so much love, that their anointing will only increase."

And this is just the beginning. God told us in Brunswick that every seven weeks we would move to a higher level of anointing. The eighth week of revival proved His words. We did, indeed, move to a higher level in God, and in the weeks that followed, many outstanding miracles would take place.

A lady who was totally blind in one eye was healed. She later came to another church where I was preaching and gave her testimony.

One of the most amazing miracles was of a twenty-year-old crippled man. He had been coming to the meetings every night to be prayed for. He was born crippled and had never walked a day in his life. When I came into the meeting one Friday recently I saw that he was up on his crutches, trying to move his feet in ways he never had before. He said he had been feeling the touch of the Lord in the meeting, and he was determined to receive his miracle.

I said to him, "Tonight, you're going to walk." I called him up during the service when the anointing was falling, and I said, "In the name of Jesus, walk! You are healed. In the name of Jesus, walk!"

He threw his crutches on the floor and began to walk. After he had taken fifteen or twenty steps, he fell down, but he got right back up and started walking again. He walked all the way back to me. This was the third totally crippled person I had seen get up and walk by God's power.

As this book goes to press, we are in our twelfth week of revival in Brunswick, Georgia, and the level of the anointing in the meetings continues to increase. We welcome all those who can to come, to experience what God is doing and to be a part of it.

This is just the beginning. God has told us that every seven weeks we will move to a higher level of anointing. The eighth week proved His words, and we are excited about what will happen next week and next month.

Chapter

Twenty-Five

"From This Generation Forever"

You, O Lord, will keep them; You will preserve him from this generation forever.

Psalm 12:7

I HAVE OFTEN WISHED THAT MY PARENTS AND GRAND-parents had lived to see this wonderful day. They loved the Lord so much and would surely rejoice in what God is doing for us now.

Daddy's death and Mama's sickness had resulted in my returning to the Lord and, as I said, Mama lived for many years afterward. One day in 1988 she told me that she had begun to long for Heaven. In a vision she had seen my Daddy, and she had seen her own parents, and a deep longing had come into her heart to meet them once again. She had lived from 1967 cancer free, but now her cancer had returned.

"Mama," I told her, "God healed you in 1967, and He will heal you again."

"I don't want to be healed this time," she answered me. "I just want to be with the Lord." And, as much as I encouraged her to fight it, she refused to resist the cancer. She was ready to go, and she wanted to go.

"If you're determined to go home," I encouraged, "that's fine, but you can go home well. You don't have to be sick. I don't want you to be sick."

She looked me right in the eye and said, "Now, you just let me handle this. Just love me and stand by me, but let me go."

Mama died at Our Lady of Perpetual Help, a Catholic home for terminally ill cancer patients. When she died, God gave me this poem:

The World's Best Mama
by Rev. Bob Shattles

Mama could touch us boys and quiet all our fear,
She'd just lay her hand on us and make our pain disappear.
She could touch a flower, and you knew that soon,

*You would see God's artwork burst into
bloom.*
She could always make worry go away,
*When she said, "Son, trust the Lord, read
the Bible, and pray."*
*Then you'd see her praying and hear, "Lord,
you're always true,*
Bless my boys, and their daddy, too."
Then total peace would come upon us,
*'Cause Mama prayed, and in the Lord
did trust.*

*When Daddy went off to fight in World
War II,*
*We were short on money, kinda lonesome
and blue,*
*But even then Mama always had the
right words:*
*"You know the Lord will feed us, He even
feeds the birds."*
*And if we got down to the last piece of pie
or cake,*
*"You boys half it, I'm full," was the excuse
she'd make.*
*When Sunday came, we didn't have to ask
where we'd go,*
*"Get ready for church, boys," and we knew
that was so!*

Pure sweet love, that's what came from Mama's heart;
That's what makes it so hard to part.
"I love you," she said, through her suffering and pain,
We knew that she meant it and that our loss was Heaven's gain.
At the last, her eyes would open, look past us to the host of angels all around,
That had come to take her to her mansion on holy ground.
Now we hear the echo of her sweet voice,
"I'll see you in the Rapture, boys,
Keep your eyes on Jesus, He's the right choice."

(In loving memory of Janice Marie Carter Shattles)

I feel very humbled that God chose our generation to display His glory in such a wonderful way. This must surely speak to us of the shortness of time and of our need to be prepared for the Lord's coming.

Chapter

Twenty-Six

"I Am There in Their Midst"

*For where two or three have gathered together
in My name, I am there in their midst.*

Matthew 18:20

WHAT IS THIS MANIFESTATION OF GOLD DUST? AND WHY
is God sending it into our midst? First, let me say
that I am personally convinced that this is not — in
any way, shape or form — what we commonly call
gold, the precious metal. The gold dust we are experiencing is something heavenly, not something
earthly. I refer to it as gold dust simply because it is
usually golden in color.

Sometimes, however, the glory that comes down
in our services like a fine mist or a misty rain is not
a golden color. Sometimes it is silver, and I have seen
it fall looking green and sometimes red.

We see the glory falling, and we see it as it lands — on people, on things, on the floor — anywhere and everywhere. It is not only happening in church services. It is appearing in people's homes and in their places of work. It appears in our automobiles, and anywhere else we happen to be at the moment.

While I do not claim that this is actually gold and have no idea what it is actually made of, I do contend that it is a divine manifestation. It cannot be explained any other way. Although this "gold" has no monetary value (that's not the purpose of it), it is far more valuable to me than actual gold or silver. The value of this "gold" is spiritual, not material.

There are several purposes for it, I believe. First, the Lord uses it to show us that He is with us, that we are His Temple, His priests and ministers. It is a sign to the world that God is real and is manifesting His presence in the world through His children.

We know that He is present with us, for He has said: *"For where two or three have gathered together in My name, I am there in their midst"* (Matthew 18:20), but He proves this to us through the manifestation of His presence.

When God's glory falls in the midst of us, people are encouraged by it and people are motivated by it. These are things that only the Lord does, so we recognize His presence in the glory. I have come to call the golden dust that falls THE FOOTPRINTS OF JESUS, for it shows where He has been.

The gold dust not only comes down as rain. It often seems to come from the very pores of the skin of the anointed. At first, it looks like perspiration. It is so oily looking, however, that it causes people to look twice and to ask questions. When the oil is wiped off, gold dust appears in its place. When it happens, I can actually smell the fragrance of the Lord, as if this miracle oil were perfumed, much like the sacred oils of the Old Testament Tabernacle.

In Brunswick, there is a lady named Amy. She and her husband have a ministry of helps, and they have been washing and ironing my shirts during the revival. She recently testified that the shirts usually have gold dust on them when she gets them. After running them through the washer and dryer, sometimes twice, the gold dust often is still there. This has shown her that it is a supernatural occurrence and that has strengthened her faith.

What does all this mean? We are often required to have important papers notarized. A notary, a recognized, respected and licensed person, places his or her signature and seal on that paper, certifying that we did indeed sign it in their presence. This is what I believe God is doing when He allows the gold dust to appear on us. He is placing His stamp on us and showing the world that we are His and that He is with us. Through the manifestation of the gold dust, God is saying, "This is real. This is mine."

As we have seen, the presence of the manifestation of God's power in our lives not only makes us
bold, but it causes men and women to listen to us. It
breaks the hardened spirits of people and causes
them to weep and fall on their knees in public places
to receive Christ as their Lord and Savior. What
could be more wonderful?

The first person we know of who received this
manifestation is a very sweet lady from Brazil. Sister Silvana came to my church earlier this year. It
would be hard to imagine a person who had suffered more physically. She was dying from cancer,
but when she was taken to a meeting with believers, God's glory fell on her, and she was gloriously
healed.

Later, gold dust began to come upon her as she
prayed and worshiped. Now it happens to her every day. When she is in a service, she rubs her hair,
and the dust, either gold or silver or platinum, literally pours out. I caught some of it in my Bible, and
it is still there many months later.

But this is not just happening in Austell or
Brunswick, Georgia or Ashland, Virginia or Brazil.
We are getting reports of it happening in many
places: California, Michigan, Indiana, Ohio, New
York, New Jersey, Canada and many places over-
seas. When my son Jim got back from his second
trip to Haiti in the past few months, he told us that

it is happening there. I can personally say that this manifestation has been witnessed everywhere I have preached in the past six months.

And this is not just happening with one person or two or three. It is happening to hundreds and thousands of people. Some of them are preachers, but many of them are lay people. Some of them are fairly well known, but many of them are not.

What a wonderful experience! It has given me a new confidence in God. As the glory dust falls on me and the supernatural oil flows from my hands, I know that when I place those hands upon the sick and suffering, they will be delivered and healed.

I know that when I begin to witness to the lost, they will listen to me, and they will listen until I have finished. Something compels them to do it.

I have had people pass me on the street, stop, turn around and come back to me, and ask, "What's that all over your face?"

I tell them, "It's the glory of God," and it gives me an opportunity to win them to the Lord.

When I go into a restaurant, people begin to look at me. They think they see something shiny and something oily too, and that gives me the opportunity to find out if they know my Lord Jesus.

I'm just a plain old Georgia country preacher, but I have tapped into something that has changed my life forever. I am having a wonderful time flowing in the river of God's glory.

If I was going to ask God for an unusual manifestation, I would have asked Him for something not nearly as messy. The combination of oil and gold dust can make a terrible mess on your clothes. But that's okay. It's a people getter. It draws them, not just because it is such an amazing sight to behold, but because there is an anointing in it that makes it hard for a lost person to say no to Jesus.

When the disciples went with Jesus up to Mt. Tabor, their lives were forever changed because *"they saw His glory"*:

> *Some eight days after these sayings, He took along Peter and John and James, and went up on the mountain to pray. And while He was praying, the appearance of His face became different, and His clothing became white and gleaming. And behold, two men were talking with Him; and they were Moses and Elijah, who, appearing in glory, were speaking of His departure which He was about to accomplish at Jerusalem. Now Peter and his companions had been overcome with sleep; but when they were fully awake, THEY SAW HIS GLORY and the two men standing with Him.*
>
> Luke 9:28-32

"They saw His glory," and that is exactly what God is doing for us today, causing us to see His glory.

We are seeing the visible manifestation of God's glory in our midst, and it is causing a seriousness among believers that we have not seen for a very long time.

God is ready to show us His glory. He is ready to reveal Himself in the Earth. He is ready to prove Himself to the world.

"Do I have to get the gold dust?" some people are asking me. No, if you don't want God's glory on you, He won't force you to have it. If you don't want a compelling anointing, He won't force you to receive it.

This reminds me of the people who used to ask me, "Do I have to speak in tongues?" No, of course not. You don't have to speak in tongues. But with this gift comes power, so why would anyone not want it?

You don't have to get in the glory. You don't have to get in the move of God. He won't force you to do anything you don't want to do. As for me, I want more and more and more, and I am not choosy about the way the Lord gives it to me. I will leave that to His discretion.

Through the visible demonstration of His glory, the Spirit of God is showing us *"things to come"*:

> *Howbeit when he, the Spirit of truth, is come,*
> *he will guide you into all truth: for he shall not*

speak of himself; but whatsoever he shall hear,
that shall he speak: and he will show you things
to come.   John 16:13, KJV

He is willing to take what is of the Lord Jesus and
to *"disclose it to you"*:

He will glorify Me, for He will take of Mine
and will disclose it to you. All things that the
Father has are Mine; therefore I said that He
takes of Mine and will disclose it to you.
                                    John 16:14-15

The Spirit of God is revealing Jesus to us. Let us
receive this revelation with thanksgiving.

Chapter

Twenty-Seven

"They Did Not Believe Them"

They went away and reported it to the others, but they did not believe them either.

Mark 16:13

NOT EVERYONE IS READILY EMBRACING THESE NEW manifestations of the Spirit. I find skeptics in every place. They are sure that if it hasn't yet happened to them, it cannot possibly be of God. I understand where they are coming from because I myself was guilty of this same type of doubt some years ago.

When laughter first began to break out in meetings here in America, I had never heard of it, so I was sure it could not be God, and I was determined not to participate in it. Rodney Howard-Browne came to Jekyl Island, Georgia for a meeting, and since I was one of the presbyters of the Fellowship of Charismatic Churches and Ministers International in the area around Altanta, I was included in the arrangements and was expected to attend.

In the Wednesday night service, everyone was laughing ... except me. On Thursday night, everyone in the place was laughing again, but I still wasn't laughing. The same thing happened in the services on Friday morning and Friday night. By then I was positive that this experience could not be God, or else it would have happened to me too.

On Saturday morning I was sitting up on the platform at the Civic Center in Jekyl with another of my fellow presbyters. He hadn't received this experience either, and we joined in our doubt of the validity of what we were seeing. I had already griped so much about what was happening that my whole staff had gone out and gotten in the van and were waiting on me there. I turned to my friend and said, "You know, Gilbert, I would believe that this is of God if He were to knock me off of this stage."

"Me too," he agreed.

When the time came for Rodney to minister to everyone, the chairs were cleared out of the way, and people began falling all over the auditorium and laughing in the Spirit. Gilbert and I just sat there on the platform looking religious. Before long, Rodney came down the center aisle, looked at the two of us and pointed his finger at us. When he did that, both of us turned over in our chairs, fell from the stage and immediately began laughing uproariously in the Spirit.

Some people wonder if these things are not faked, but who is going to fake falling from a stage onto a concrete floor from a distance of four feet? In that moment, I had to repent and recognize that the laughter had been of God all along. I just hadn't moved into it sooner.

I guess one of the reasons I had been skeptical was that I had never read in the Bible about Jesus or His disciples having a laughing fit. I knew that Jesus had wept because there were people He wanted to do things for, and they refused to get involved, they wouldn't press in. But did He laugh?

Then, one day God spoke to me from the book of John:

> *Therefore many other signs Jesus also per-formed in the presence of the disciples, which are not written in this book.*   John 20:30

When I read that, I lost all my doubts and have not questioned the Lord again on these matters. If He wants to send laughter, so be it. If He wants to send gold dust, I am ready for His will. If He wants to send supernatural oil, I refuse to question His reasoning. I am going to enjoy everything that God does for me and not worry about those who can't accept it.

Some are terrified that they will receive something that is not of God. I personally cannot share that fear. I am positive that it is impossible for us to call upon the name of the Lord and receive something that is undesirable. He taught this clearly in His Word:

> *If a son shall ask bread of any of you that is a father, will he give him a stone? or if he ask a fish, will he for a fish give him a serpent? Or if he shall ask an egg, will he offer him a scorpion? If ye then, being evil, know how to give good gifts unto your children: how much more shall your heavenly Father give the Holy Spirit to them that ask him?* Luke 11:11-13, KJV

When we seek the Lord, He makes sure we receive something good.

Some Christians are waiting for many confirmations before they join in the new things that God is doing. I personally don't need for an angel to come down and confirm to me what is or isn't of God. I'm walking with the Lord, and He can tell me Himself. Jesus and I talk. We're friends. We get along with one another, and I trust Him.

Why is it that when we are praying for a move of God and it comes, we decide that it can't be from Him, and we refuse to cooperate with it? This is a trick of the enemy. It is time to jump into God's river and to receive all that He has for us.

Some believers are very frightened of looking foolish. During the sixteen years I served with the Atlanta Police Department, I did some mighty stupid things. I am ready to do some peculiar things for the Lord now — if that's what it takes for men and women to get saved.

When we were out drinking and carousing in the world, we didn't worry about what we looked like. Why is it that now when God is doing great things in us, some people worry constantly about what they look like? When we were in the world and acted like fools, we even laughed and bragged about it. Now, when the power of God comes on us, we are embarrassed and don't want anyone to see us that way. Why is that?

"Me, slain in the Spirit, lying on the floor, talking in tongues?"

"Me, touched by the Spirit, running through the sanctuary?"

"I don't want anybody to see me like that."

Well, if we're going to look foolish, let's look foolish for the Lord. It's okay to act crazy for God. It's time to lose your fears and come out of the camp of the skeptics.

We are so vain about our appearance that we lay in the sun or under a tanning bed to achieve a tanned and healthy look, but when God wants to place upon our countenances the look of Heaven, we somehow find that hard to accept. Why is that?

God knows how to deal with skeptics. Friends of mine recently told me of a meeting they conducted in a church in the South. The pastor and his staff were highly skeptical of what God was doing, so God did something for each of their homes. The pastor's wife, the worship leader's wife and the staff evangelist's wife all went forward for prayer. Gold dust was falling, golden oil was flowing from their hands, and people were receiving gold fillings in their teeth.

The following day these three ladies wanted to testify. They said that they had each received gold fillings. God was saying to those men, "If I can't convince you, I will convince your wife, and maybe she can convince you." I hope those men lost their doubts.

There are always some skeptics around, and skeptics don't bother me. Many people are skeptical about salvation. Others are skeptical about the baptism of the Holy Ghost. Others are skeptical that the laying on of hands and healing are for us today. You can always find skeptics, and they were present in Jesus' day as well.

The enemies of Jesus didn't get stirred up until He began to walk in the power of the Holy Spirit and do signs and wonders and miracles among the people. From then on, some of the scribes and Pharisees followed Him around, trying to find a way to disprove His teachings. At one time, they even credited the work the Spirit was doing through Him to the devil. Jesus warned them not to blaspheme against the Holy Ghost. There would be no forgiveness of it, He said, *"in this age or in the age to come"*:

> *"Whoever speaks a word against the Son of Man, it shall be forgiven him; but whoever speaks against the Holy Spirit, it shall not be forgiven him, either in this age or in the age to come.*   Matthew 12:32

It is one thing to be skeptical because something is new, but when we begin to blaspheme the Holy Ghost, we are treading on dangerous territory.

Please be slow to judge anything new that is happening in the Christian world. What you are labeling false may be part of the true move of God. Be slow to judge it and criticize it. You are not speaking against a man or a movement, but against the Spirit Himself.

One night while the oil was flowing in the meetings in Michigan, a lady was singing. God showed me that she was sick and that if she would allow me to lay hands on her and pray for her, she would be healed. I sensed, however, that she was bound by tradition and might not accept my ministry.

Sure enough, when I told the lady what I felt led to do, she turned very pale and refused to allow me to lay my hands on her. She said she had every confidence in the doctors and would trust them to diagnose her sickness and treat her. Cases like that break my heart, and I'm doing everything I can to help people be free from traditions that rob them of God's very best for their lives.

Jesus showed us that if we cling to tradition, our tradition makes the Word of God *"of no effect"* (KJV). We have *"invalidated the word of God"*:

> *And by this you invalidated the word of God for the sake of your tradition.* Matthew 15:6

Jesus called people who do that *"hypocrites"* (Verse 7) and said that their worship was *"in vain"* (Verse 9). I don't want to be any part of that group, and I hope that you don't either. I made a determination long ago to be willing to let go of any tradition that would interfere with what God was doing in my life. Please make that same commitment today.

Don't doubt God. Don't doubt what He is doing. Open your heart to Him. When we turn His Holy Spirit away, we are turning Him away. When we don't like His manifestations, we limit His presence in our lives.

Forget about how things are normally done in your church and in your denomination, and let God have His way with you and with your ministry. This is a new day. Forget the way you did it yesterday. Let God show you new ways, His ways.

If we don't get out of our little pattern of behavior and open up to new things, God will move on past us. He is coming for His one glorious Church, and if we are not part of that one glorious Church, we will surely be left behind. Some think there will be other opportunities, but I can't take that chance. I want to go on the first busload. I want to rise with that first trumpet blast. I want to go up with that first shout. When He says come forth, I want to be ready.

Why is it that some people don't want to humble themselves and say, "Please lay hands on me, I need this"? Pride is a destructive force. It will keep you from God's very best for your life.

The attitude we find in some is:

"I've got it all already."
"If I don't have it already, it must mean that I don't need it."

"If God wants me to have it, He'll give it to me."

I find that kind of thinking to be hard to understand. The lady in the Bible who received healing for her issue of blood had to press through the crowd to get to Jesus, and I am determined to touch the hem of His garment too. I want to be close to Jesus, and I want to get closer and closer to Him as it comes nearer to the time that I will live with Him forever.

I want to get as many people saved as I can, so I want to let them see God's glory. I don't want the blood of lost souls on my hands. I don't want to fail in my duty of telling men and women about Jesus.

I love the Lord, and I certainly don't want to be an extremist in a worldly sense, but I don't mind being an extremist for Him. I want to be radical about His cause.

It will take a radical move of God to attract our teenagers back to the church and back to God. They are waiting on that to happen and, when it comes in all its force, it will shake this generation and cause America to turn back to God.

Revival is here, and America will be changed forever. Prayer and Bible reading will be returned to their rightful place in our society, but it will happen through the revelation of the glory of God, not through any other means.

Like Moses, I am ready to turn aside and see the

bush burning. Every single day, I say to the Lord, "Dear God, I want to see the bush burn today."

Every day He answers me, "If you will let it burn, I will set it on fire. If not, you won't see it."

God was angry with the children of Israel in the wilderness and rebuked them for their stiffnecked attitude and their hardheartedness. He hates pride, and He can't stand proud people. He can't stay around the unbelieving.

When God promised Moses to lead him forth into the promised land, He said He didn't want to go with him because He couldn't stand the attitude of the people. Moses cried out to the Lord and asked Him what it would take to have Him with them. He couldn't think of going on without the presence of the Lord, and I feel exactly the same way.

I want to know what I have to do to have God's presence with me today and tomorrow and next week and next month. I want to see His glory manifested in every service I am in. I want to see His glory as I travel and as I rest. And He will only manifest His presence with us as we humble ourselves, remove fears and doubts from our hearts and believe Him.

Finally, I would say to every skeptic: before you judge this thing that God is doing, stop and look at the fruits. Jesus said:

> *You will know them by their fruits. Grapes are not gathered from thorn bushes nor figs from thistles, are they? So every good tree bears good fruit, but the bad tree bears bad fruit. A good tree cannot produce bad fruit, nor can a bad tree produce good fruit.*   Matthew 7:16-18

The fruits of this ministry are that thousands of people are being saved, thousands are being healed and thousands are being delivered. Hundreds of pastors are finding a brand new ministry. What could be more wonderful?

It is important that you not be skeptical of this experience, for if you harbor doubts, you certainly will not receive it. I can lay hands on people and nothing will happen unless they are hungry and open and receiving. You cannot be skeptical and have God's glory on your life.

The same Spirit who was with Jesus when He did so many signs that they could not all be recorded in the Bible is still with us, and He is still doing signs and wonders today, many of which we have never seen before.

I would say to pastors: Put aside all your fears. Fear is not of God. Stop caring what others will say about what you do in God. Just worry about what God says about you. If you will let God decide your future for you, He will send you power to back up everything you do and to make your life and ministry fruitful.

God is trying to show us that He is alive, that He is real and that His Spirit is taking of Him and showing it unto us to prepare us to live with Him forever. He is clothing us with His glory. Let Him do it.

Chapter

Twenty-Eight

"The Glory of the Lord Will Be Revealed"

Then the glory of the LORD will be revealed,
And all flesh will see it together;
For the mouth of the LORD has spoken.

Isaiah 40:5

WHO NEEDS THIS GLORY OF GOD? FROM WHAT WE HAVe seen, it should be obvious that we all need it. Without the power of God in our lives, we are nothing, and we can do nothing. A humorous story from my life in police service illustrates the point.

My partner Sam and I were called one night to a bar along the river called Johnny's Place. Sam was the biggest, baddest man on the entire force. He was a "pulpwooder" from Alabama, and as long as he was my partner, nobody dared messed with us. If

Sam couldn't take care of someone, however, we were in serious trouble.

When we got to Johnny's Place, the owner, was waiting out front for us. He said, "Tiny Tim is in there, and he's tearing my place up. I want you all to take him out of there."

I knew the man he was talking about. Tiny Tim was well known in the area. He was six-four or six-five and weighed about two hundred and eighty or ninety pounds, and his body was like solid steel. When he was drunk, nobody wanted to mess with him.

I went in and confronted the man. "Come on, Tiny," I said, "we've got to go."

"I ain't goin' nowhere," he snarled.

I said, "Look, you're either going to come, or we're going to take you."

"I ain't goin' nowhere," he repeated.

Sam was just coming in the door, and I said, "Get him, Sam."

Sam got him on one side, and I got him on the other, but Tiny flung his arms outward, and, when he did, I hit one wall, and Sam hit the other wall.

"We've got a problem," I said to Sam.

We had our badges on, and they identified us as people of authority. We had the necessary authority, but Tiny didn't seem to understand that. He wasn't cooperating.

"Tiny," I said, "stop resisting us. You're going to get yourself in serious trouble. Let us take you out of here."

"If you gonna take me, you gonna have to take me by force," he insisted.

So we ran at him again. This time he slung me, and I went flying out the front door. I was just trying to get up and go back in when Sam came skidding out after me. We looked at each other and realized it was time for some serious persuasion. We had the authority, but we also had the power. It was in the holster on my belt.

I pulled out my pistol and cocked it, went back in and put that gun right under Tiny Tim's chin. Then I said to him, "Tiny Tim, if you hit me one more time, I'm going to blow your head off."

"Hey man," he said, "I don't want no trouble," and the incident was ended.

This is a true story, and the point I want to illustrate with it is that we need God's power to enforce the authority we have been given.

We are trying to take back what the devil has stolen from us, we're trying to heal the sick, and we're trying to win the lost, yet we don't seem to have time to pray or time to worship God. We rush about from activity to activity, and are much too dignified to let God pour out His glory on us, too proud to get into His river and let Him carry us away. So what should we expect?

Some wonder why nothing is happening in their personal life or in their ministry. I wonder why anything at all is happening with Christians who have no time for the glory of God. Without God, nothing good can happen.

God's Kingdom is a kingdom of power, so why are so many of us powerless?

A man came to the disciples of Jesus and asked them to cast a spirit out of his son, but they could not do it. God was not lacking in power, but they were. They didn't have enough of God in them at the moment to get the job done. We need more of His presence, more of His power. I have often said that some of us don't have enough of God's anointing to pull a sick hummingbird off its nest.

Jesus said to His disciples:

> *O unbelieving generation, how long shall I be with you? How long shall I put up with you? Bring him to Me!*   Mark 9:19

This was a very desperate case, and these people needed help.

> *They brought the boy to Him. When he saw Him, immediately the spirit threw him into a convulsion, and falling to the ground, he began rolling around and foaming at the mouth.*

> *And He asked his father, "How long has this*
> *been happening to him?" And he said, "From*
> *childhood. It has often thrown him both into*
> *the fire and into the water to destroy him. But*
> *if You can do anything, take pity on us and*
> *help us!"*   Mark 9:20-22

If anybody ever needed help, these people did, yet the disciples, who were supposed to be walking with Jesus, didn't have the power to do anything about it. That's sad.

Jesus showed that it was not a question of His ability:

> *And Jesus said to him, " 'IF You can?' All*
> *things are possible to him who believes."*
>   Mark 9:23

Jesus had already given the disciples authority over all the power of the devil, but when we have the authority, we also need the power that goes along with it.

The great Smith Wigglesworth had twelve or fifteen people raised from the dead during his ministry, and he was a great soul winner. We spend far too much time devising programs to get the job done. We have notebooks full of jottings from the many seminars we have attended on church growth. We have stacks of unread books on the subject. And still not much is happening. It is time to get into God's river. It is time to say, "God, give me Your glory."

Jacob was changed by his encounter with God at Bethel, when he held onto God until God blessed him, and that is exactly what will change your life and my life today.

God is still no respecter of persons, and what He does for one, He will do for all. He can change our homes; He can change our churches; He can change our ministries; and He can change our meetings. Even if we have experienced a measure of success in the past, the presence of God's glory with us can cause us to change entire communities where we live and minister.

It is time that we let God move, that we stop hindering Him, that we stop fighting Him, that we stop resisting Him. It is time that we stop criticizing others and judging them. It is time to become a willing vessel in the hands of the Lord and let Him use us mightily to bring honor to Himself. It is time to allow Him to reveal His glory on our behalf.

A small boy appeared at a church one day while the service was going on. Approaching one of the ushers, he said, "Can I see the pastor?"

"Well, the pastor's getting ready to preach," he was told. "This is not a good time to see him."

"I really need to see him," the boy said. "It's a matter of life and death."

The usher led the boy to one of the pastors, and when he was asked what he needed, he said, "I need to know if God is here today."

"What do you mean?" the pastor asked.

I mean, "Did God come to church here today?" the boy insisted.

"Well, we certainly hope so," the pastor replied. "He comes here every day. Why do you ask?"

"I've got to know," the boy insisted. "The doctor just left our house, and my mama is dying. The doctor said there was nothing more he could do, that it's all up to God now. Can you ask God to help my mama?"

That simple request from a small boy rocked that church. Those people got on their face before God and repented of anything they had done to keep Him from the service that day. Then they all prayed together and asked God to touch the boy's mother.

By the time the boy got back home, his mother was up and dressed and preparing him a meal. The last time I heard she was still living.

That's why we need the power of God.

Jesus promised us:

> *Behold, I have given you authority to tread on serpents and scorpions, and over all the power of the enemy, and nothing will injure you.*
>
> Luke 10:19

That's why I need God's power. Make a decision this day to get anything and everything out of your life that stands between you and God, between you and His glory, so that you can be more effective in His Kingdom. If you would you like to have this power today, please pray this prayer with me now:

Father,

We are tired of the devil having more power then we Christians. You promised us power through the Holy Ghost, and You said that with that power we could be witnesses. Your power in us is to cause men and women to come into Your Kingdom. Make us witnesses today, I pray, by the mighty power of Your Spirit.
May all those who are hungry for a move of Your Spirit — all those who are hungry for lost souls to be saved, all those who are hungry for a river to flow in their church, in their home, in their town ... may they now get into the flow of Your great river of glory.
We believe You for it this day, and we dedicate ourselves to walk in it.

In Jesus' name,
Amen!

Chapter

Twenty-Nine

"Your Soul Is Required of You"

But God said to him, "You fool! This very night your soul is required of you; and now who will own what you have prepared? So is the man who stores up treasure for himself, and is not rich toward God."   Luke 12:20-21

One Saturday morning, as I got out of bed, a certain police lieutenant I had worked with came to my mind. I had not seen nor talked with him in twenty years. He had given me a hard time when I left the police department to go into the ministry, but I didn't hold it against him. I considered that I probably deserved it for the kind of life I had lived among my peers before I recommitted my life to Christ.

All day that day I could not get this man off my mind, so I finally called him. His wife answered, and I asked her how they were doing. She said that he had cancer, and that there was no hope for him. "Time is running out for him," she said, "and he knows it."

I asked if I could speak with him, and he got on the phone. We talked a little about the police department, and then he said, "I don't know any preachers, and I'm dying. Will you preach my funeral?"

I told him I would and asked him if he was ready to die, if he was saved. He began to weep and said, "No, I don't even know how to get saved."

I asked him if he knew who Jesus was, and he told me that he did. I asked him if he believed that Jesus died on the cross for all who would allow Him to take away their sins, and he said he did. I asked him if he believed that Jesus rose from the grave and ascended into Heaven, and he said he did. I led him in a sinner's prayer. He wept, and his voice broke, as he prayed for Jesus to come into his heart and save him.

The man thanked me over and over again for caring enough to call and help him. We buried him a few days later, and I was able to tell his family that by God's grace, through Jesus Christ, their loved one was very much alive, healed and happy with Jesus.

Although it is very dangerous to wait to be saved until you are on your deathbed (and I do not recommend it), it worked for that man.

Not every case ends so satisfactorily. One Sunday morning, as I was preaching, I saw a police sergeant come into the church and sit down on the very back pew on the left side. I preached that day on salvation, and when I gave the altar call, I saw him step out into the aisle several times as if he was about to come forward, but he never came.

After the service ended I was at the front door of the church, speaking to people as they left. This police sergeant was the last to leave that day. Tears were streaming down his face, as he said to me, "I needed to be saved."

"Why didn't you come on down?" I asked.

"Because I'm still living in sin," he said.

I explained to him that Christ died for sinners, not for the just. I gave him the Bible promise:

> *But God demonstrates His own love toward us, in that while we were yet sinners, Christ died for us.*   Romans 5:8

I went on to explain to him the entire plan of salvation. I told him that salvation did not come because of any good works we do, but because of God's grace. When I tried again to get him to accept the Lord right there on the steps of the church, he said, "I can't right now. I'll come back next Sunday."

The next morning someone called me from the hospital and asked if I could come to the morgue and identify a body. They thought he was an Atlanta police officer, they said, and they needed positive identification. When the cart was rolled out, and the sheet was pulled back from the cadaver, I stared down into the face of the man who said he couldn't accept Christ "right now," that he would come back the next Sunday. He would never get that chance now. His life was over.

He had been crying on my church steps the day before and said that he knew he needed to be saved. Still he wanted to wait for another time. Well, that "other time" would never come now. The final bell had tolled in his life, and there were no more chances.

This man had the mistaken idea that he had to "make things right" before he could get saved. It's the other way around. Getting saved gives us the power to set things right in our lives. Jesus accepts us just as we are, and then He makes something different of us. He takes us, torn and bruised and battered and yes, full of sin, and He makes something beautiful of our lives. This man somehow apparently had not understood that fact.

"What happened to him?" I asked the doctor.

"He was in a car wreck last night and was thrown out and killed instantly. He never knew what hit him."

"I hope he at least had time enough to call on Jesus," I said through my tears.

The doctor wept with me as he closed the vault and we walked out of the morgue. "Me, too," he said.

If you have never been saved, and you feel like you need to be, realize that Jesus died to take away your sins. He rose from the grave and showed Himself to many. Then He ascended into Heaven to sit on the right hand of God the Father. He is there to make intercession for you. Ask Him to come into your heart today and to forgive you of your sins. Ask Him to save you and to become the Lord of your life.

Pray this prayer with me now:

Dear Lord Jesus,

I realize that I am lost. I believe that You died for my sins and that You were raised from the dead. I invite You to come into my heart. I confess that You are my Savior and ask You to be Lord of my life.

In Jesus' name.
Amen!

If you feel that you need help finding the Lord, please feel free to write or call me, and I will be happy to pray with you.

If you prayed and asked Jesus to save you, go to church next Sunday and tell the pastor what you did. Follow this decision up by being baptized in water and go on to all the other great blessings God has for your life.

Chapter

Thirty

"How Great Is Your Goodness"

How great is Your goodness,
Which You have stored up for those who fear
You,
Which You have wrought for those who take
refuge in You,
Before the sons of men!   Psalm 31:19

SOMETIMES, IN THE MIDDLE OF ALL THAT GOD IS DOING, I stop and look around me, and invariably I begin to weep as I consider the greatness of it all. This happened to me again just recently. I saw myself as I had been before I met the Holy Spirit and before the visible manifestation of His glory came into my life, and I can say that I was a very different man, a man without a clear vision, a man without excitement.

When this manifestation of God's glory began last November, I had no outside meetings booked. Our church was doing well enough that I was going out only a few days each year. Since this began, however, I haven't stopped traveling. This blessing has affected our church (we have reached a membership of two thousand, six hundred and growing, and we have been forced to buy additional property in Cobb County to accommodate our ministry), and I have had the joy of taking this glory out to many other places and to many other people.

My life today is extremely exciting. I live in constant expectation of what God is going to do next. What an honor God has bestowed on me! What undeserved favor!

I have so much to be grateful for. As I continued to look around me that day, I saw my wife Mary. She is my strength. She stands behind me and supports me as my best intercessory prayer warrior. I have many voluntary intercessors who lift this ministry up before the Lord, and they are scattered from Canada to Florida and from Georgia to California, but Mary is always at the top of the list.

Mary is heavily involved in our praise and worship and has a unique anointing for playing and singing. She also "holds down the fort" when I have to go away, as I have so much recently. She not only takes care of our family, she watches after many aspects of our ministry. God knew what He was doing when He gave me a woman like her. I could never repay her many kindnesses. I am her pastor and her husband, but we are also best friends and have become much closer through this revival of the glory of God.

When this blessing first came to us, she was very supportive, saying to me, "Let's go for it. Let's go all the way. Let's press in. Let's let God do what He wants to do." For that, I am extremely grateful.

What a precious pastor's wife she is! I am so thankful to God for healing her of cancer in 1985. It was a wonderful witness to everyone who knew her. Words fail me to express how much I appreciate her and what God has done in her life.

I saw Robyn that day. God brought her back from sure death, and she is now leading our praise and worship team and playing the keyboard. Such a heavenly talent! She has a deep dedication to serve the Lord. While others have come and gone, Robyn has remained devoted and faithful and consistent. I know that I can depend on her because she never makes excuses. I am proud to be her Daddy, and I am proud to have her involved in my ministry.

I saw my grandson Paul Hicks, Robyn's son, playing the drums in our church. We would not have him if God had not healed his mother when she was at death's door. At fifteen, he is a great big fellow, and his heart is just as big as he is. I saw the glory of God all over him. He had golden oil on him, and golden rain was falling all around him. I sensed that God has a great future for his life.

When this blessing first came to us, Robyn and her husband Gene Wray and Paul got in right away and began flowing in it as well. Our entire family had a new vision for the Lord.

I saw Jim that day, as he prayed and worshiped God, with his wife Angie and my granddaughters, Heather, Brooke, Alicia and Ashley, at his side. I quietly thanked God again for bringing him back into the fold after he had strayed for several years. He and Angie jumped into the anointing and began flowing with it.

I saw my special adopted daughter, Roxanne, and her husband Danny in their regular place with Danielle.

I saw Bill, and his wife Reba as they faithfully served God with us.

I saw all of my church family, loving one another, as we prayed, praised, worshiped and served together. For sixteen years, the Lord had been supplying our every need, and now He was lifting us into ever higher levels of His anointing. What a blessing! How great is the goodness of the Lord!

I saw that God had extended our family far beyond the borders of our own church. I thought of Pastor Bill and Mrs. Dorothy Jean Ligon who have been so gracious to host the revival in Brunswick at Christian Renewal Church. I knew that the glory was falling even when I was not there because Pastor Ligon has the same anointing. I was grateful to them for being such devoted pastors and for having opened their doors to revival.

I thought of the worship team leaders at Christian Renewal Church, Mack and Alyson Tucker. Night after night, they had been there to do what God had called them to do, to lead us in worship into the very throne room of God.

I thought of the other members of the praise teams with which we are blessed both at Friendship Baptist Church and Christian Renewal Church. God was using them to carry His revival forth, and I was sure that a great reward awaited them, each one, in Heaven.

I thought of Pastor Kevin Drury and his wife Donna, who had been so very faithful. God had given him the anointing, oil was flowing from him, and gold dust was showing up on him.

I thought of men who helped me consistently and tirelessly around the altars, men like Dominick Zangla and Kelly Medders. They not only help me as I minister to people. Dominick also blows his *shofar* and inspires the people. They go out and witness and invite people to come to the revival, and they go out and teach and preach and lay hands on the sick. How blessed I was to have men like these by my side!

I thought of the debt of gratitude I owed to Sister Ruth Heflin for obeying God and coming to my church. I was grateful that the anointing that was on her had been transferred to me. The gold dust and the oil had not failed in a single service in any city since the day God had given me this anointing. It was there consistently, day in and day out.

I thought of all the pastors and evangelists and teachers who had come to hear me preach, and I was grateful that God had used me to transfer this blessing to them as well.

I thought of the radio and television programs on which I had been interviewed in recent months and the many people who had called in and been blessed.

Yes, I had much to be thankful for. No wonder I wept for joy that day, as I have many times in recent months!

It was all very humbling. I know that I am nothing, that I am no different than others. I am just as human as any other man. But I told God that He could use my life any way He wanted, and He heard my cry.

I am determined never to lose the humility God has given me and that I will never allow doubt or unbelief or skepticism to come in and rob me of His blessings. I want Him to use me in these last days in which we live.

I pray that God will allow the gold dust and the anointing of glory it represents to continue to draw the lost to Him. I pray that He will allow the supernatural oil and the healing power it represents to continue to bring healing to the sick and deliverance to the captives.

To everyone who reads this book I want to now say: God is not playing favorites by blessing Friendship Baptist Church, the people of Brownsville, Toronto, Ashland, Brunswick or any other place where revival has broken out. He will manifest Himself in your church and in your city if you will let Him do it.

Why not give the Holy Spirit a try in your life? The blessing of the Spirit is part of God's promise to you, and His Word will stand forever.

I am praying for you that God's will be done in your life, and I stand willing to help you with revival in your city and your church. If you would like for God to do a new thing in your life, get down on your knees before God right now, lift up your hands to Him and say, "God, I know that I am nothing. I am just a humble vessel. Use me in any way that You desire." He will do it for you TODAY.

As you pray, let a little gold dust come upon you.

Let a little supernatural oil come into your hands, and your life and ministry will be changed forever.

Please pray with me now:

> Lord,
>
> *Send down Your Holy Ghost fire.*
> *Send it down, and let us see it.*
> *Send down Your golden glory Lord.*
> *Send down Your gold dust.*
> *Send down the supernatural golden anointing oil.*
> *Lord, let us see that great move of Your Spirit that Joel foresaw coming in these last days. You promised that You would pour out of Your Spirit upon all people and, Lord, I believe it.*
> *I believe it! I believe it! And I believe it is for us today, for every single person who will receive it.*
> *Let it happen this day.*
>
> *In Jesus' name,*
> *Amen!*

And He [Jesus] said to them, "Go into all the world and preach the gospel to all creation. He who has believed and has been baptized shall be saved; but he who has disbelieved shall be condemned.

"And these signs will accompany those who have believed: in My name they will cast out demons, they will speak with new tongues; they will pick up serpents, and if they drink any deadly poison, it shall not hurt them; they will lay hands on the sick, and they will recover."

So then, when the Lord Jesus had spoken to them, He was received up into heaven, and sat down at the right hand of God. And they went out and preached everywhere, while the Lord worked with them, and confirmed the word by the signs that followed.   Mark 16:15-20

About the Author

Dr. J. Robert Shattles, Sr. attended John Marshall University Law School (1963-64), graduated from the University of Louisville in Louisville, Kentucky, with a degree in Police Administration and Science (1967), from Kennesaw College in Marietta, Georgia, with an Associate degree in Science (1974), from the Southern Baptist Center in Jacksonville, Florida, with a Bachelors degree in Ministry (1983) and from Jacksonville Theological Seminary in Jacksonville, with a Masters degree in Counseling (1992) and a Doctors degree in Theology (1993).

He was the founder of Teens Set Free, a youth ministry that he directed in the Atlanta area from its inception in 1967 until 1975. He organized and served on the Board of Directors of Christian Police Officers in Atlanta (1973).

He is a volunteer chaplain for Parkway Medical Hospital in Douglas County, Georgia and for Cobb Medical Center in Cobb County, Georgia.

He has been the chaplain for the Cobb County, Georgia Police Department from 1977 until the present. He also serves as chaplain for the Cobb County Sheriff's Department and the Austell, Georgia Police Department.

In 1973 he received the Lion's Club Citizenship Award for his contribution to the welfare of the community.

He participated in the Billy Graham School of Evangelism (Memphis, Tennessee — 1978; Florida, West Coast — 1979; and Nashville, Tennessee — 1979).

He was director of evangelism for the Concord Association from 1977 to 1982.

He is a member of the Kennesaw College Alumni Association, the Jacksonville Theological Seminary Alumni Association and a charter member of the American Association of Christian Counselors. He has been a member of the Fellowship of Charismatic Churches and Ministers International since 1987. In 1990, he became a presbyter for that group in the Atlanta area and served as their president from November of 1990 until October of 1993.

He was a member of the steering committee for the Pentecostal Fellowship of North America Conference in Atlanta in 1993.

He was elected to serve on the Board of Trustees of Mountain Foreign Missions, Inc. (1997).

He is the Senior Pastor of Friendship Baptist Church in Austell, Georgia and Friendship Baptist Church in Douglasville, Georgia, with a combined enrollment of two thousand, five hundred members.

Services are conducted at Friendship Baptist Church in both Austell and Douglasville, Georgia every Sunday at 10:30 a.m. and 6:30 p.m. Every Wednesday at 7:00 p.m. the church meets for its "Holy Ghost Fire" night. "Holy Ghost Fire for Teens" meets every Tuesday night at 7:00 p.m. at the Austell location. Both congregations welcome you to join them for these services. (Call to confirm days and times of meetings.)

Pastor Bob Shattles and the members of his staff are available for revivals. They may be contacted at the following address:

Friendship Baptist Church
1880 Old Alabama Road
Austell, Georgia

Telephone 770 941-9407
Fax 770 941-4783

Additional copies of this book may be purchased at your favorite bookstore, from the publisher, or by writing, calling or faxing this same address.